RUTH WEBB LEE'S HANDBOOK

MAGNET AND GRAPE WINE JUG, INSCRIBED IN GILDED LETTERS, "TRY ME"

RUTH WEBB LEE'S HANDBOOK

OF EARLY AMERICAN PRESSED GLASS PATTERNS

CHARLES E. TUTTLE COMPANY
Rutland, Vermont & Tokyo, Japan

REPRESENTATIVES:

For Continental Europe:
BOXERBOOKS, INC., Zurich

For the British Isles:
PRENTICE-HALL INTERNATIONAL, INC., London

For Australasia:
BOOKWISE, Beverly, South Australia

Published by the Charles E. Tuttle Company, Inc.
of Rutland, Vermont and Tokyo, Japan
with editorial offices at
Suido 1-chome, 2-6, Bunkyo-ku, Tokyo

Library of Congress Card No. 84-52146
International Standard Book No. 0-8048-7005-5

Copyright, 1936, 1946, by Ruth Webb Lee
Copyright, 1964 by Robert W. Lee
© 1984 by Charles E. Tuttle Co., Inc.

First Tuttle edition 1984

Printed in USA

IN EXPLANATION

It is not so many years ago that collectors of American blown glass and writers on the subject attached little importance to the later commercial glassware which flooded our markets during the decades preceding and following the Civil War. Collectors of rarities found little pleasure in acquiring anything so plentiful as glass made in America from 1840 to 1890. But the urge to buy essentially American antiques grew stronger year by year, and with it a broader view of the desirability of securing what would harmonize with furnishings in the creation of an entirely American atmosphere in the dining room Today discriminating collectors are as keenly interested in matching sets of this popular glass, both crystal and colored, as they used to be in acquiring the rare forms of blown glass.

Ever increasing demand necessitated a standard nomenclature for early American pressed glass. It was a source of annoyance and expense both to collectors and dealers to find that different sections of the country had different names for the same pattern. No collector could be certain that if he ordered Baltimore Pear from Ohio he would receive what Pennsylvania or Connecticut dealers knew by that name. But even more deplorable was the fact that many attractive patterns were virtually uncollectible by mail because they had no name at all. Descriptions and rubbings did not always prove successful in obtaining matched specimens for the amateur who wanted to complete a set of the pattern of which the trade name had been lost and no substitute agreed upon.

Realizing the urgent need of a common language on the subject led me to attempt what had been declared by some editors and writers to be an impossible feat; namely, to classify the myriad designs of glass produced in a highly commercialized era; that is, from 1840 through the '70's and '80's.

Early American Pressed Glass was released to an eager group of glass lovers. From the first, collectors and dealers, as well as librarians, accepted the book as the standard authority. It established once for all a nomenclature and it gave the first accurate classification of the hundreds of patterns and forms that are collectible.

In Explanation

Only a pioneer book on a given subject can bring to light material which was unobtainable at the time the manuscript was written. Letters from interested readers poured in and resulting research brought out a large number of old trade catalogues, thereby affording information on when, where and by whom many of our popular designs were made. As a result of these valuable discoveries, it was deemed advisable to revise and enlarge *Early American Pressed Glass*. This revised edition was published with valuable new material.

During the ensuing twelve years the intensive search for our old American pattern glass was so great that designs which were comparatively common when my first volume was written, became not only rare but much higher in price. It was decided to revise and enlarge *Early American Pressed Glass* a second time, thereby bringing it up to date. New illustrations have been included as well as additions to classifications.

The constantly increasing interest in *Early American Pressed Glass* indicates no abatement in the demand for accurate information on the part of an ever-growing horde of collectors. These same collectors, as well as countless dealers, asked for sets of the photographs and line drawings used in my book, to carry with them on their travels. *Early American Pressed Glass*, with its 712 pages, is too heavy to take about handily. It is therefore the purpose of this Handbook to serve as an indispensable guide to old pattern glass, affording a means of identifying patterns, alike to dealers and collectors on collecting trips as well as to those who do not own *Early American Pressed Glass*.

For the benefit of the novice, it might be noted here that beginning with the publication of *Early American Pressed Glass*, all designs identified in this and subsequent books of the author, are universally recognized as "Lee" patterns. Eagerly sought, they represent the best in their period.

RUTH WEBB LEE

INTRODUCTION TO THE NEW EDITION

The Ruth Webb Lee books are so well-known and so universally acknowledged to be the best in their field they need no introduction. However, I should like to mention what I consider to be my mother's most remarkable time-proven accomplishment. The Ruth Webb Lee books cover a specific time prior to 1900. The material covered in her books is so complete that the period covered remains up-to-date without need for revision.

I have been asked, "How did your mother ever assemble the glass for the photographs, research the material and find time to write her books?" My answer is brief and to the point. It took many years of unceasing devotion and hard work.

A prominent collector once commented, "Having this book is the next best thing to owning the glass itself." This book was written for collectors, museums, dealers and all who love and appreciate early American glass.

I sincerely hope this book will bring you pleasure and the information you seek.

Robert Webb Lee

PLATE 1—GOBLETS

Ashburton
Flute

Loop
Excelsior

PLATE 2—GOBLETS

Colonial
Argus

Crystal
Mirror

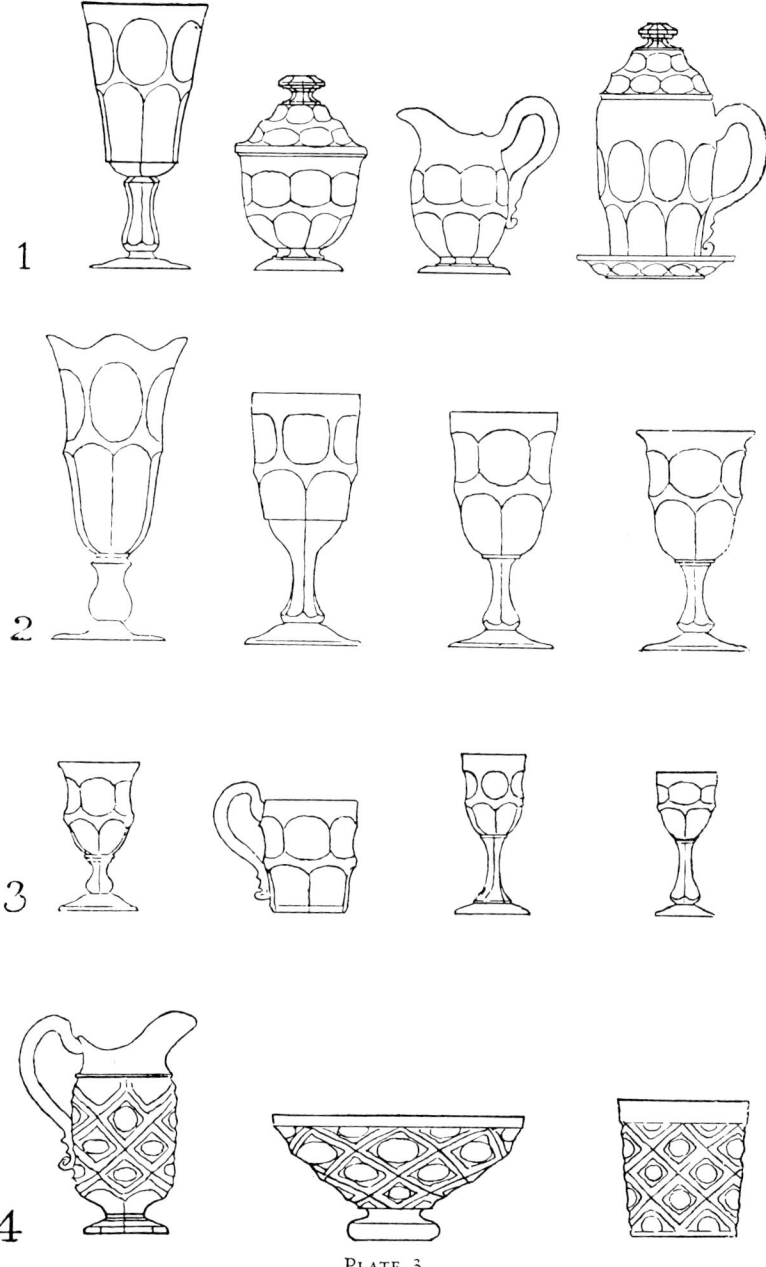

PLATE 3
1. ASHBURTON celery vase, sugar bowl, creamer, toddy glass with plate.
2. ASHBURTON celery vase, goblet with disconnected ovals, goblet in usual form, goblet with flaring bowl.
3. ASHBURTON egg cup, handled mug, wine, cordial.
4. DIAMOND THUMBPRINT creamer, bowl with low foot, tumbler.

PLATE 4
1. EXCELSIOR goblet, footed tumbler, double egg cup, egg cup.
2. EXCELSIOR tumbler, wine, cordial, claret.
3. LOOP covered compote on high standard, deep plate, covered bowl.
4. PETAL and LOOP open compote, sugar bowl, sauce dish.

PLATE 5—EUGENIE PATTERN
Reproduced directly from page of old trade catalogue, McKee & Brothers, Pittsburgh, Pa.

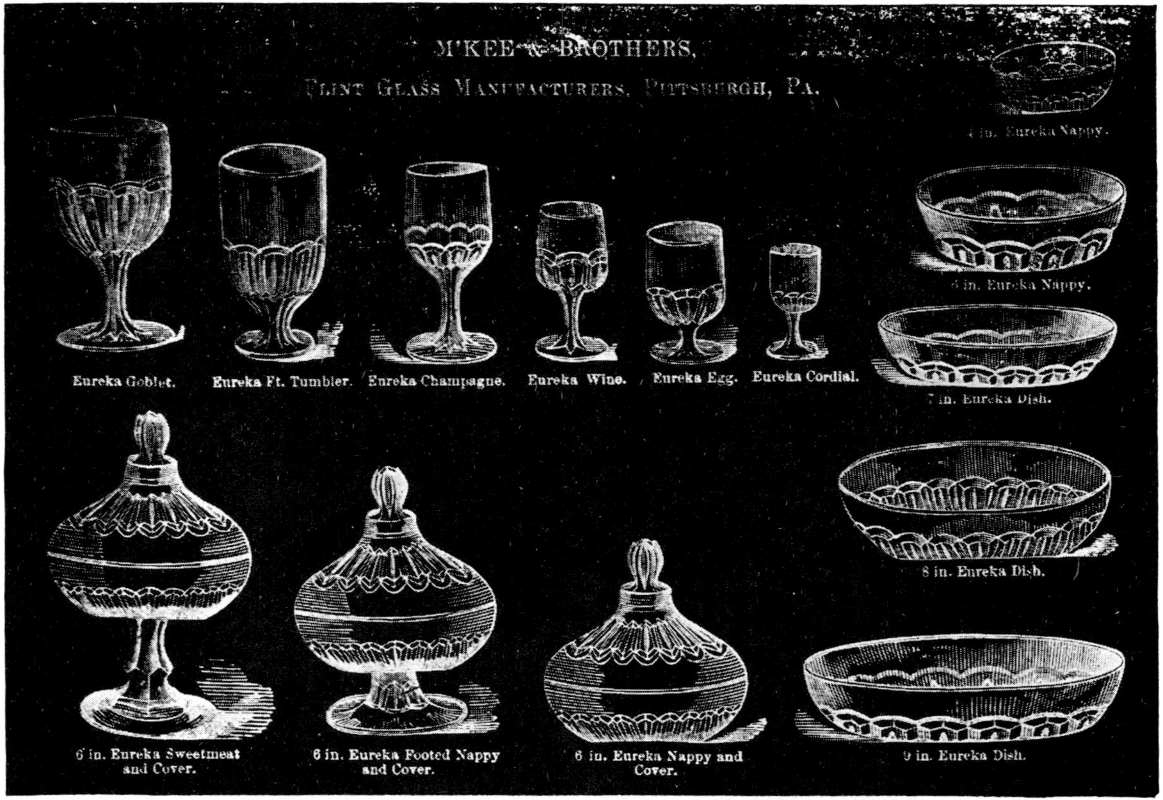

PLATE 6—EUREKA PATTERN

Reproduced directly from page of old trade catalogue, M'Kee & Brothers, Pittsburgh, Pa.

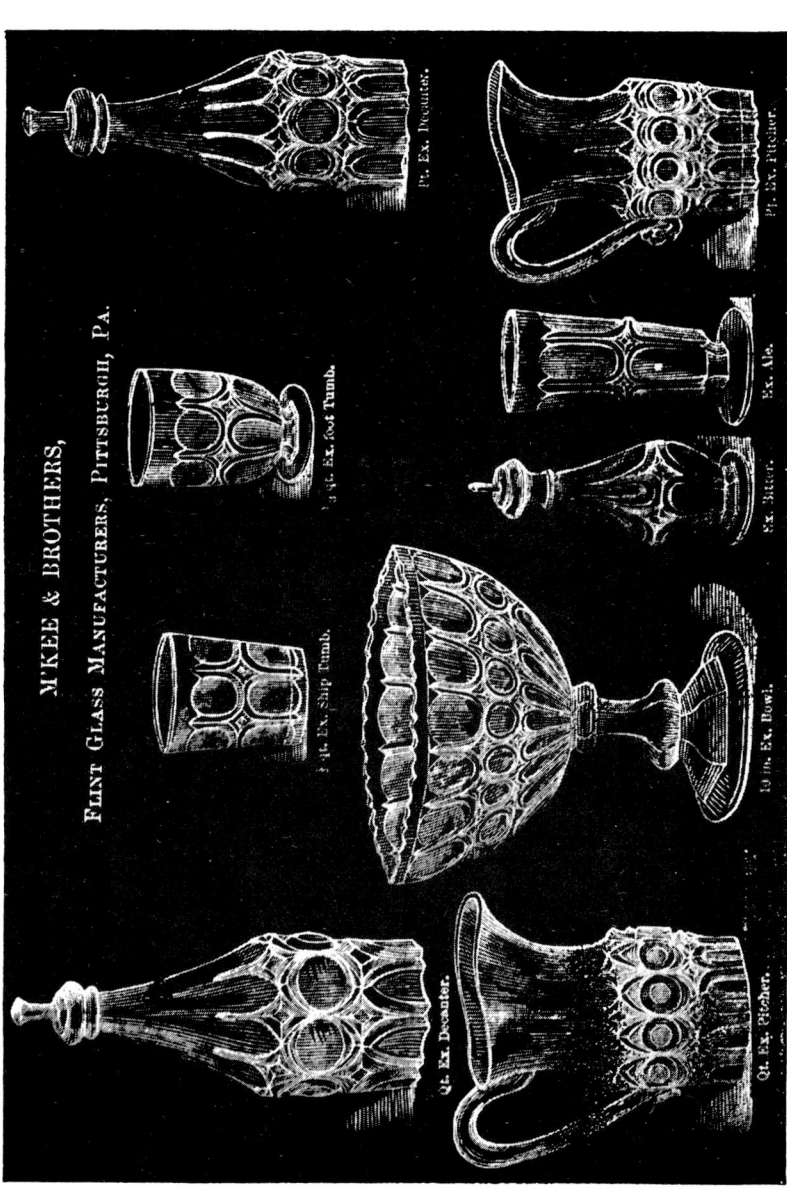

PLATE 7—EXCELSIOR PATTERN
Reproduced directly from page of old trade catalogue, M'Kee & Brothers, Pittsburgh, Pa.

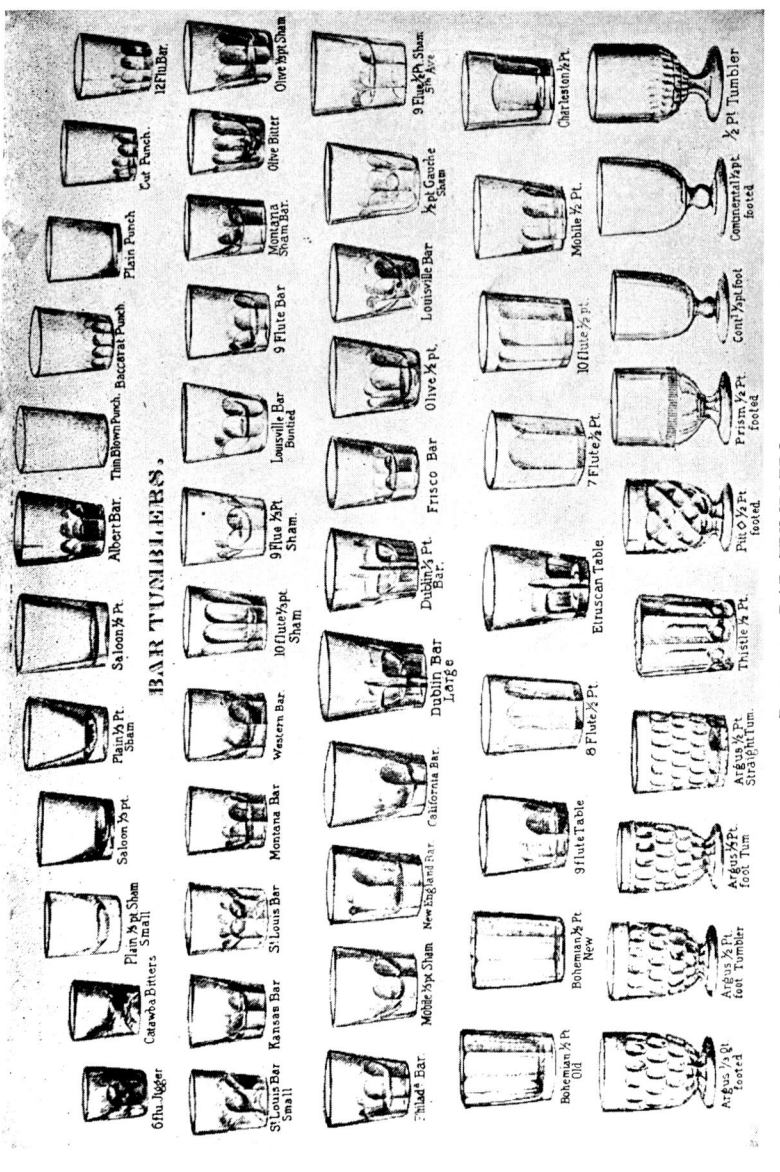

PLATE 8—BAR TUMBLERS

Reproduced directly from page of old trade catalogue, Bakewell, Pears & Co., Pittsburgh, Pa.

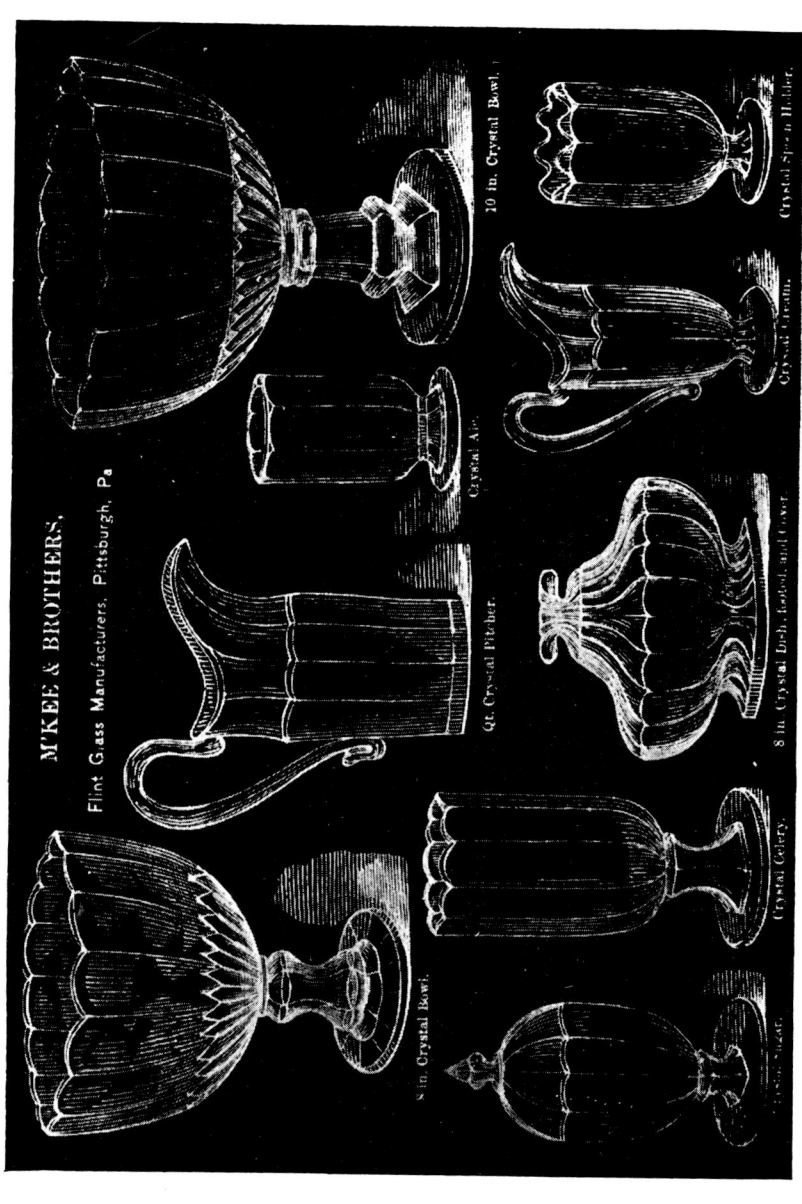

PLATE 9—CRYSTAL PATTERN

Reproduced directly from page of old trade catalogue, M'Kee & Brothers, Pittsburgh, Pa.

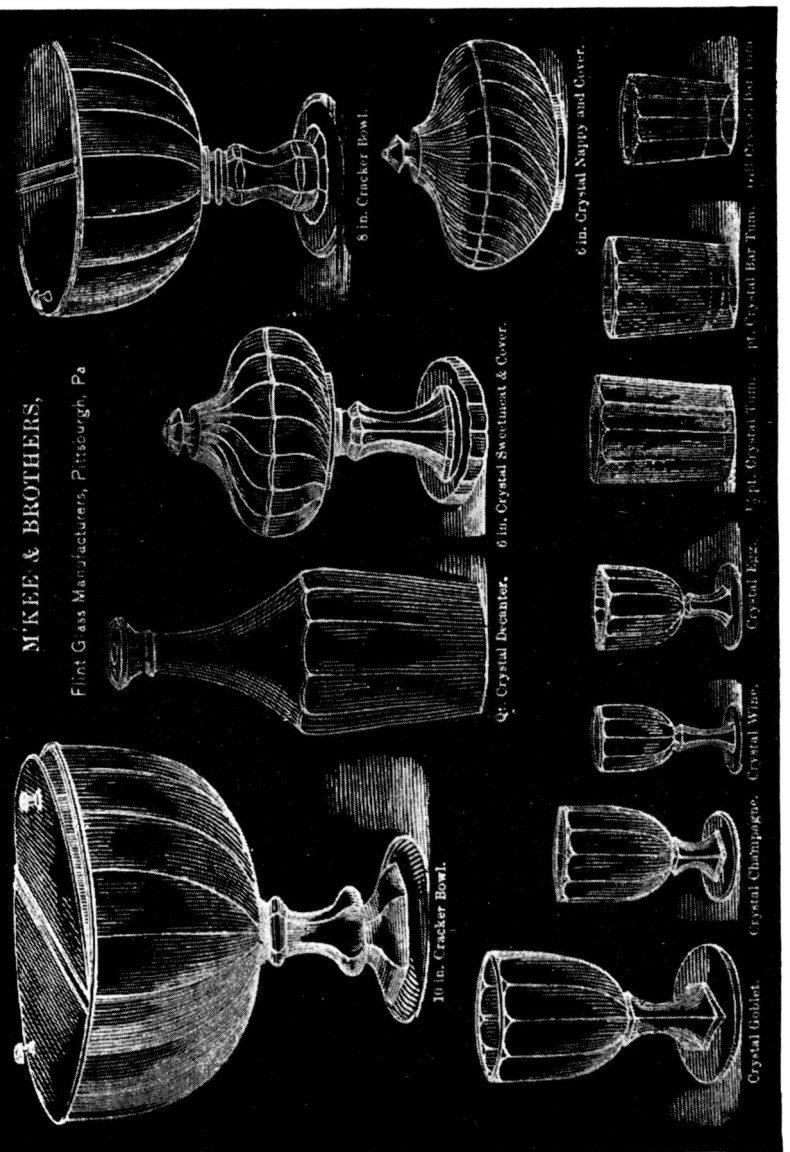

PLATE 9A—CRYSTAL PATTERN
Reproduced directly from page of old trade catalogue, M'Kee & Brothers, Pittsburgh, Pa.

PLATE 10
1. WASHINGTON water pitcher, decanter with original stopper, decanter with bar lip.
2. COLONIAL sugar bowl, goblet, ale glass.
3. WAFFLE and THUMBPRINT decanter with patent stopper, cordial, compote, spoonholder or spill holder.
4. BIGLER goblet, tumbler, cordial

PLATE 11
1. ARGUS sugar bowl, lamp, ale glass.
2. ARGUS champagne, wine, cordial, whiskey tumbler, handled mug.
3. HUBER compote on high standard, compote on low foot, egg cup, handled egg cup.
4. HUBER sugar bowl, creamer, celery vase.

PLATE 12
1. FOUR PETAL sugar bowl, creamer, sugar bowl, with rounded lid.
2. PRESSED BLOCK compote, covered bowl, covered compote.
3. OVAL MITRE compote, oval dish, goblet.
4. SUNBURST plate, celery vase, egg cup, wine glass.

PLATE 13
1. BLAZE goblet, sugar bowl, creamer, spoonholder.
2. STEDMAN decanter with bar lip, syrup pitcher, goblet, egg cup, cordial.
3. PRISM decanter with bar lip, water pitcher, goblet, egg cup, cordial.
4. FLUTE syrup jug, goblet, champagne, wine.

PLATE 14
1. SANDWICH STAR decanter, goblet, spoonholder.
2. HARP spoonholder, handled lamp, footed salt.
3. RAY plate (six inch), sugar bowl, celery vase.
4. ENGLISH HOBNAIL and THUMBPRINT bowl, fruit dish, sauce dish.

Collection of Mr. E. B. Merrill.

PLATE 14A

Extremely rare Sandwich Star compote, with triple-dolphin standard, usually found on Sandwich glass lamps

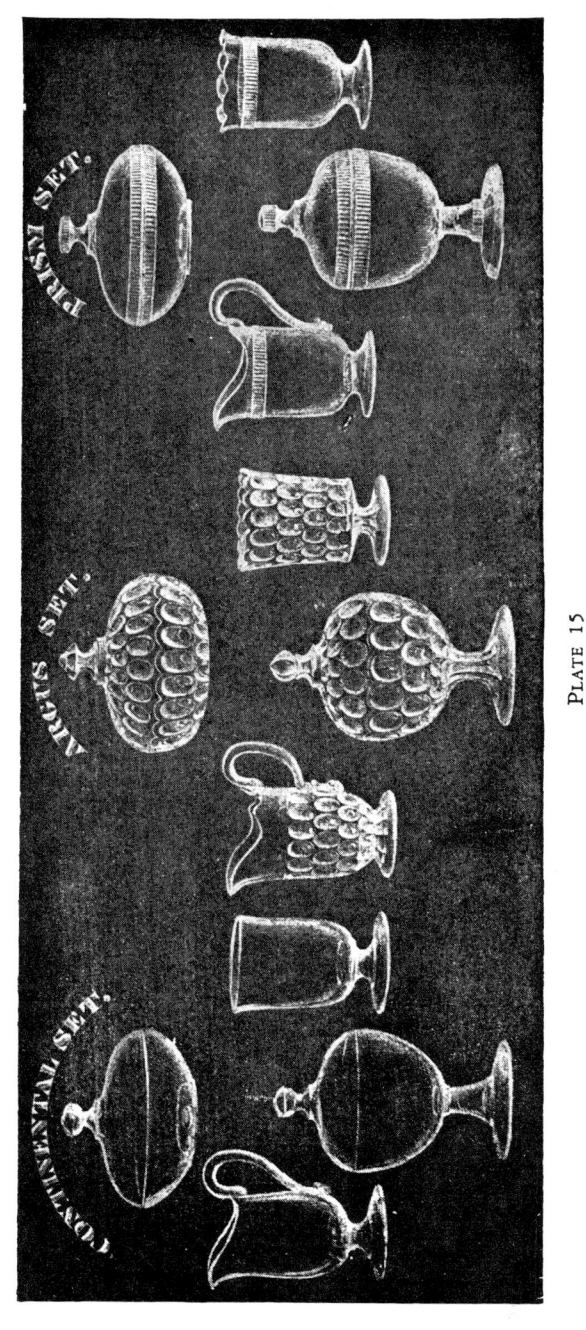

PLATE 15

Page from Bakewell, Pears & Co., catalogue, showing "sets" of Continental, Argus (now known as Thumbprint) and Prism (now known as Prism and Flute).

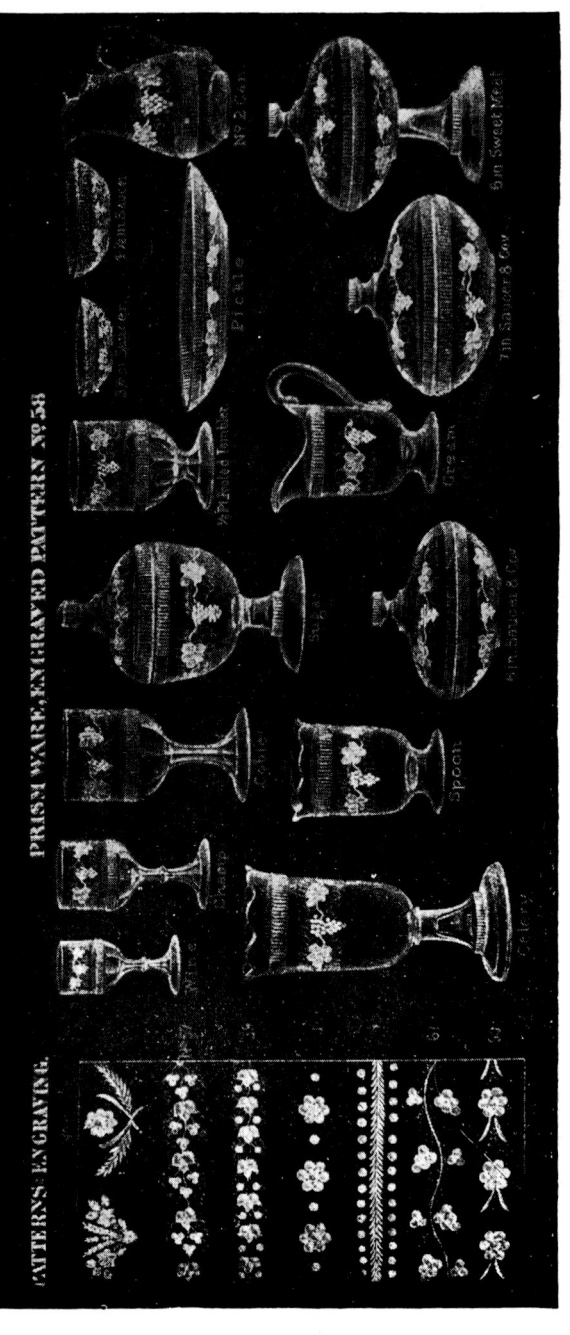

PLATE 16

Page from Bakewell, Pears & Co. catalogue, showing "Prism" pattern (Prism and Flute), engraved, together with patterns used for engraving.

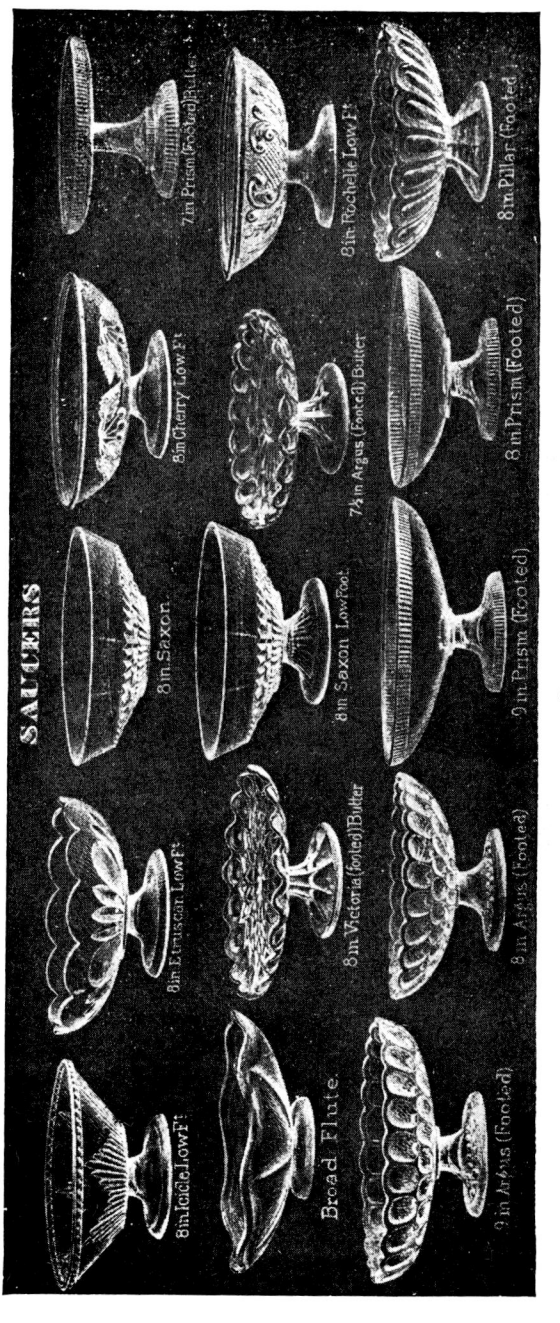

PLATE 17

Page from Bakewell, Pears & Co. catalogue, showing their "saucers" and footed butter dishes.

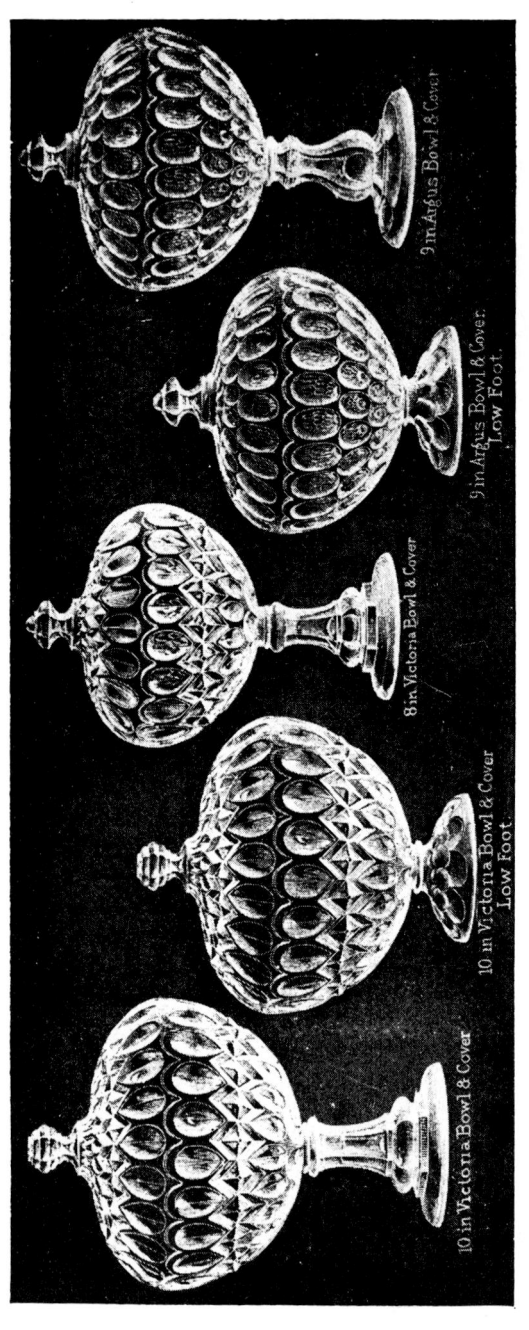

PLATE 18

Group of covered compotes in the Victoria and Argus patterns, of the Bakewell, Pears & Co. (Argus is now known as Thumbprint).

PLATE 19

"Sets", showing Rochelle, Icicle and Cherry patterns, taken directly from an old trade catalogue of Bakewell, Pears & Co., Pittsburgh, Pa. (Rochelle is now known as Princess Feather).

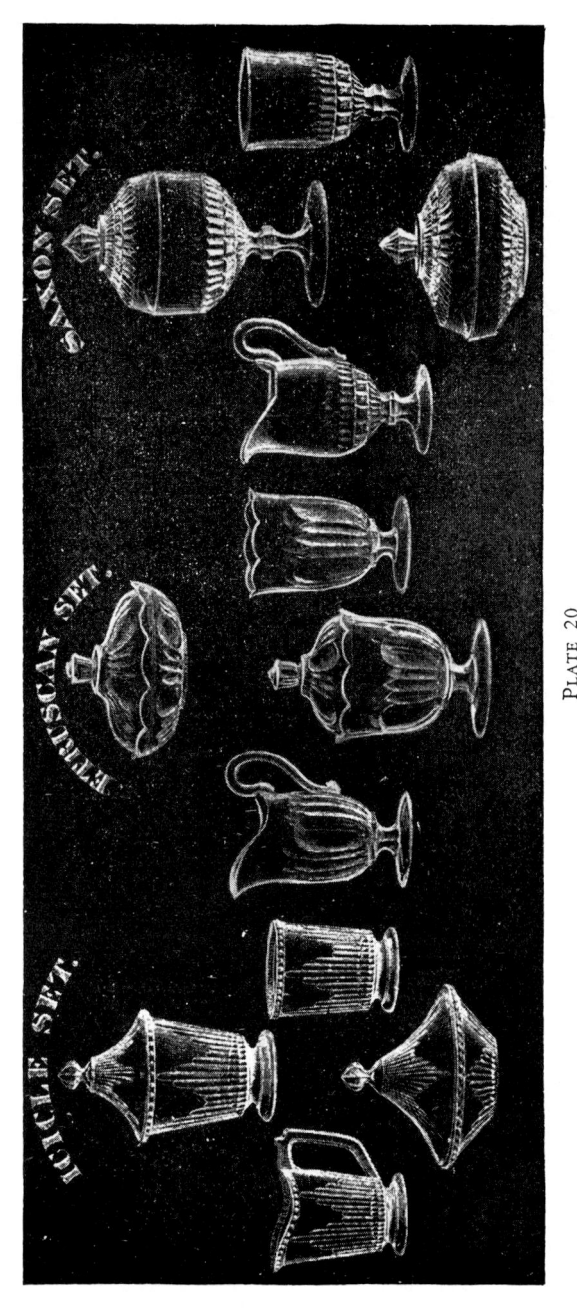

PLATE 20

"Sets" showing Icicle, Etruscan and Saxon patterns, taken directly from an old trade catalogue of Bakewell, Pears & Co., Pittsburgh, Pa.

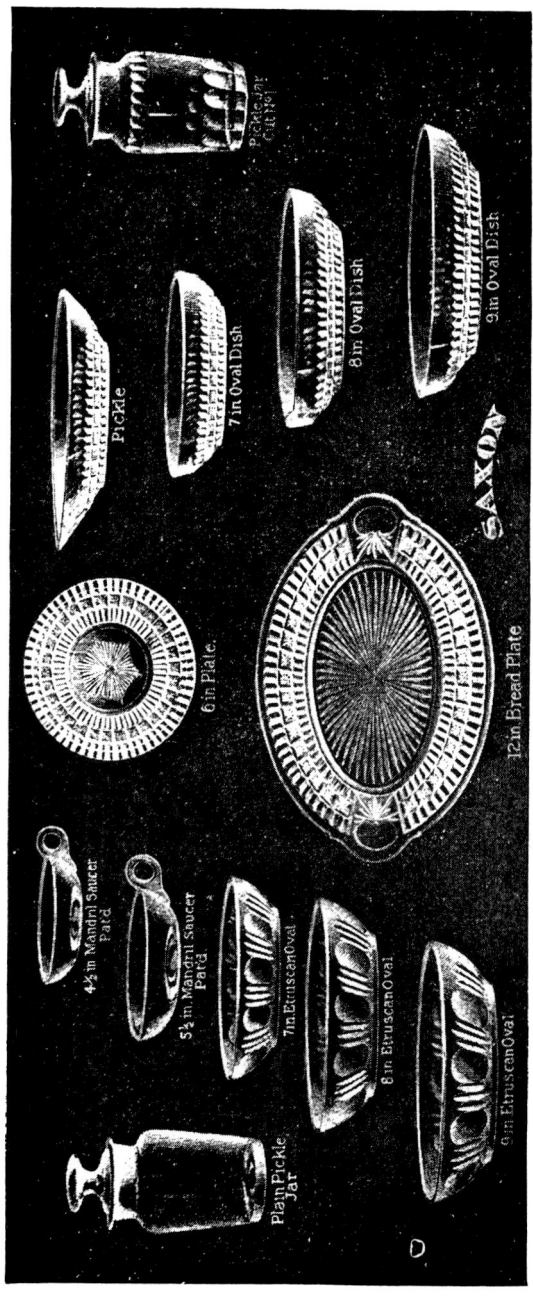

PLATE 21

Page taken from Bakewell, Pears & Co., trade catalogue, illustrating Saxon pattern.

PLATE 22

Group of Icicle pattern and Dolphin dish, as taken from an old trade catalogue of Bakewell, Pears & Co., of Pittsburgh, Pa.

PLATE 23

Group of covered dishes, taken from old trade catalogue of Bakewell, Pears & Co, Pittsburgh, Pa.

PLATE 24

Group of goblets, in patterns made by Bakewell, Pears & Co., carried on both early and fairly late.

PLATE 25
Diamond Thumbprint
Popcorn Pattern

PLATE 26—GOBLETS

Waffle and Thumbprint Cube
Lincoln Drape Lincoln Drape with Tassel

PLATE 27—GOBLETS

Bull's Eye with Diamond Points Ribbed Grape
Prism Fine Rib

PLATE 28—GOBLETS

Stippled Medallion Arched Leaf
Pillar Variation of the "Pillar"

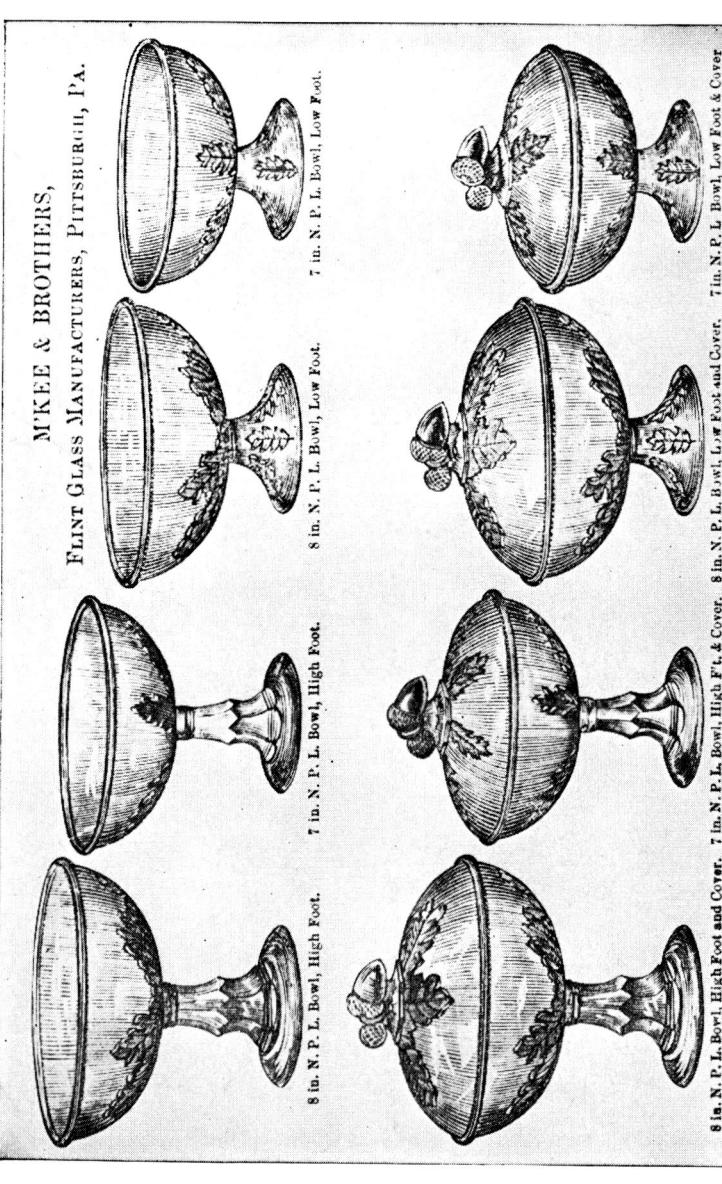

PLATE 29

Group showing the "N. P. L." pattern of M'Kee & Brothers, as shown in their trade catalogue. This pattern is now known as Pressed Leaf.

PLATE 29A

Group showing the "N. P. L." pattern of McKee & Brothers, as shown in their trade catalogue. This pattern is now known as Pressed Leaf.

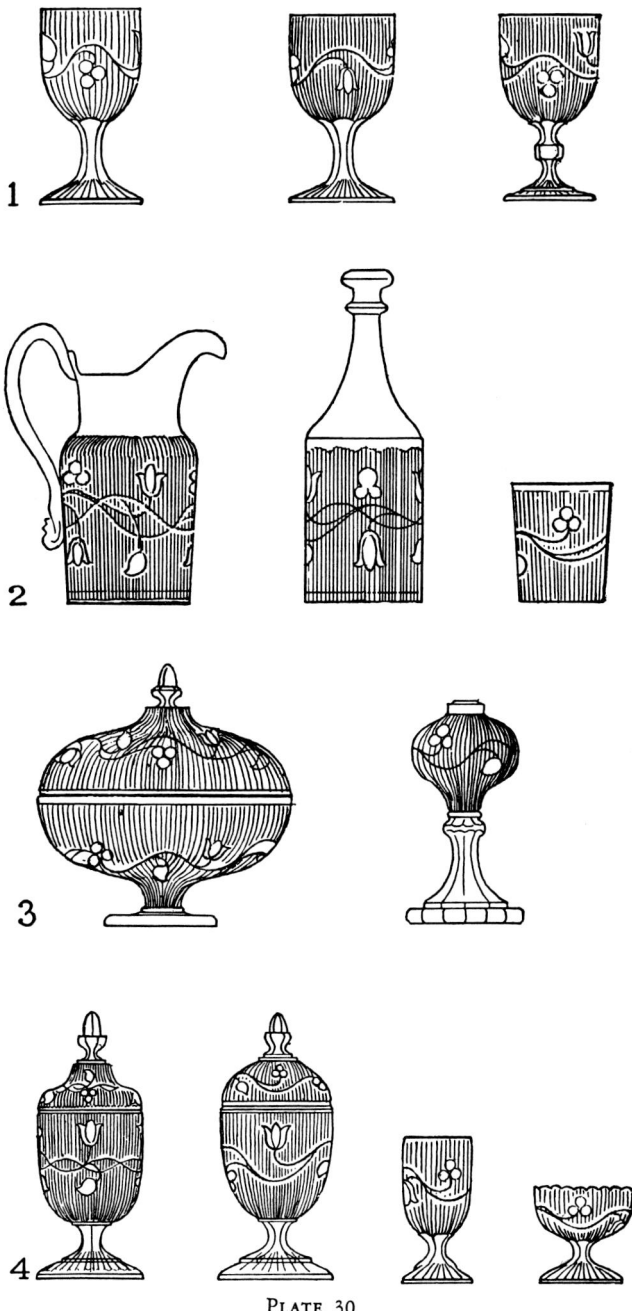

PLATE 30
1. BELLFLOWER goblet with coarse rib; barrel-shaped goblet with fine rib; barrel goblet, fine rib, knob stem.
2. BELLFLOWER water pitcher with double vine; decanter with double vine and bar lip, tumbler.
3. BELLFLOWER covered compote on low foot, lamp.
4. BELLFLOWER sugar bowl with double vine; sugar bowl with single vine, egg cup, salt.

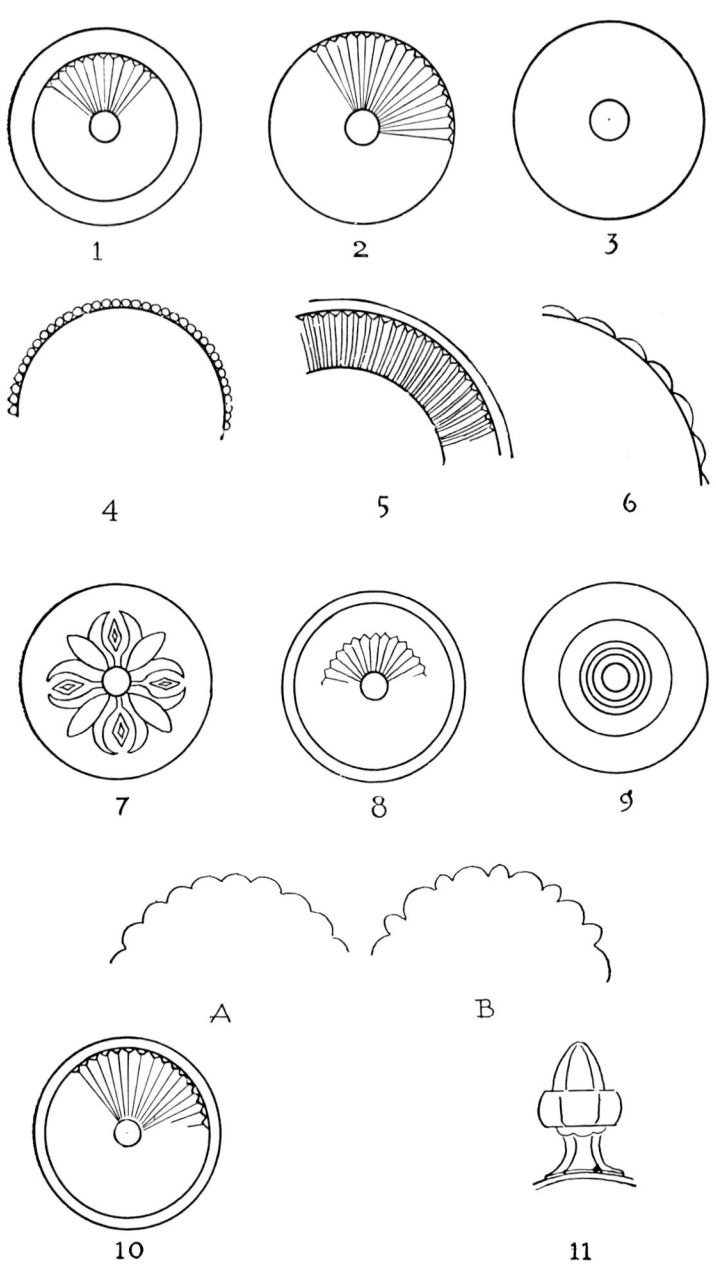

PLATE 31—BELLFLOWER DETAILS

PLATE 31A
Rare octagonal Bellflower sugar bowl, of Midwestern origin.

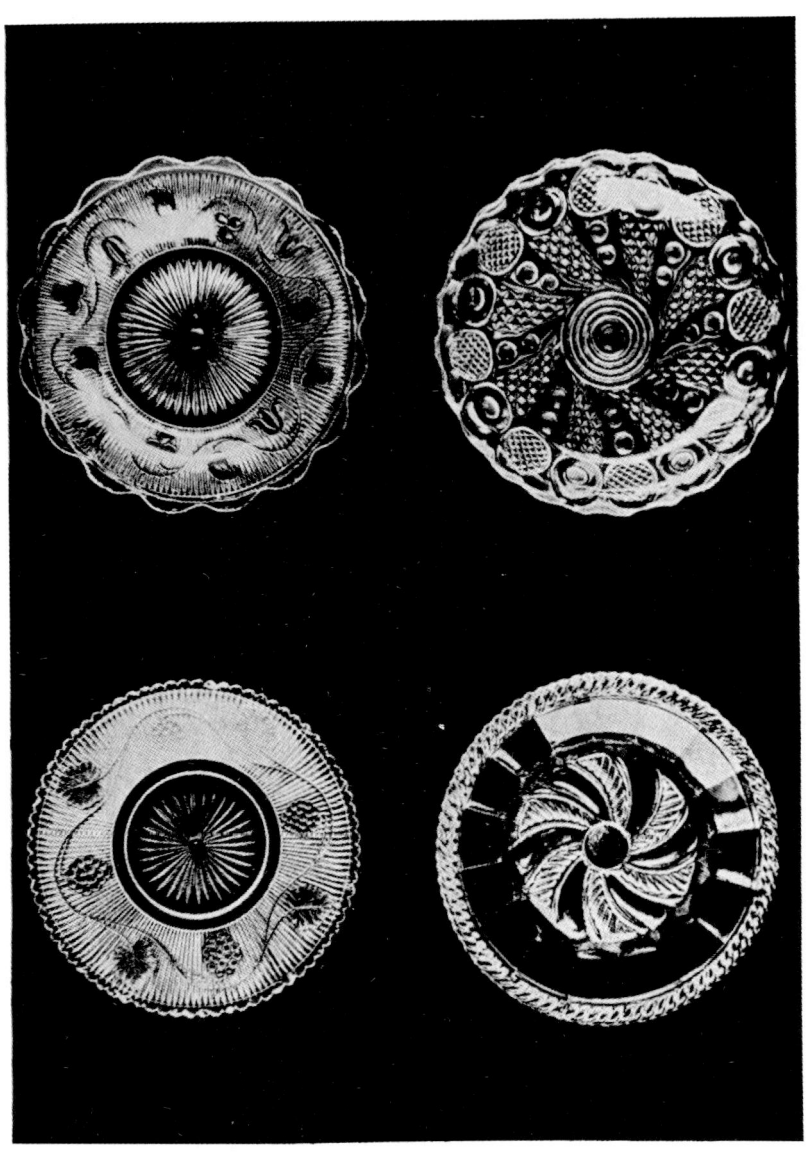

PLATE 32—SIX INCH PLATES

Bellflower
Ribbed Grape

Horn of Plenty
Cable

PLATE 33—GOBLETS

Ribbed Ivy
Ribbed Palm

Bellflower
Inverted Fern

PLATE 34
1. BELLFLOWER castor set in pewter standard, celery vase, footed tumbler.
2. RIBBED VARIANTS of BELLFLOWER ERA, cut against a fine rib background.
3. Candlesticks in EXCELSIOR pattern. One of the earliest pressed glass designs to match table ware. Found in two sizes.

RIBBED GRAPE COMPOTE   OPAL BELLFLOWER EGG CUPS

PLATE 55

PLATE 36
1. RIBBED GRAPE creamer, sugar bowl, spoonholder.
2. FINE RIB goblet, covered compote on low foot, footed salt, cordial.
3. INVERTED FERN sugar bowl, butter dish, egg cup, sauce dish.
4. CABLE goblet, open compote, footed salt, egg cup.

PLATE 37—SIX INCH PLATES

Tulip
Ribbed Palm

Waffle
Rayed, with Loop border

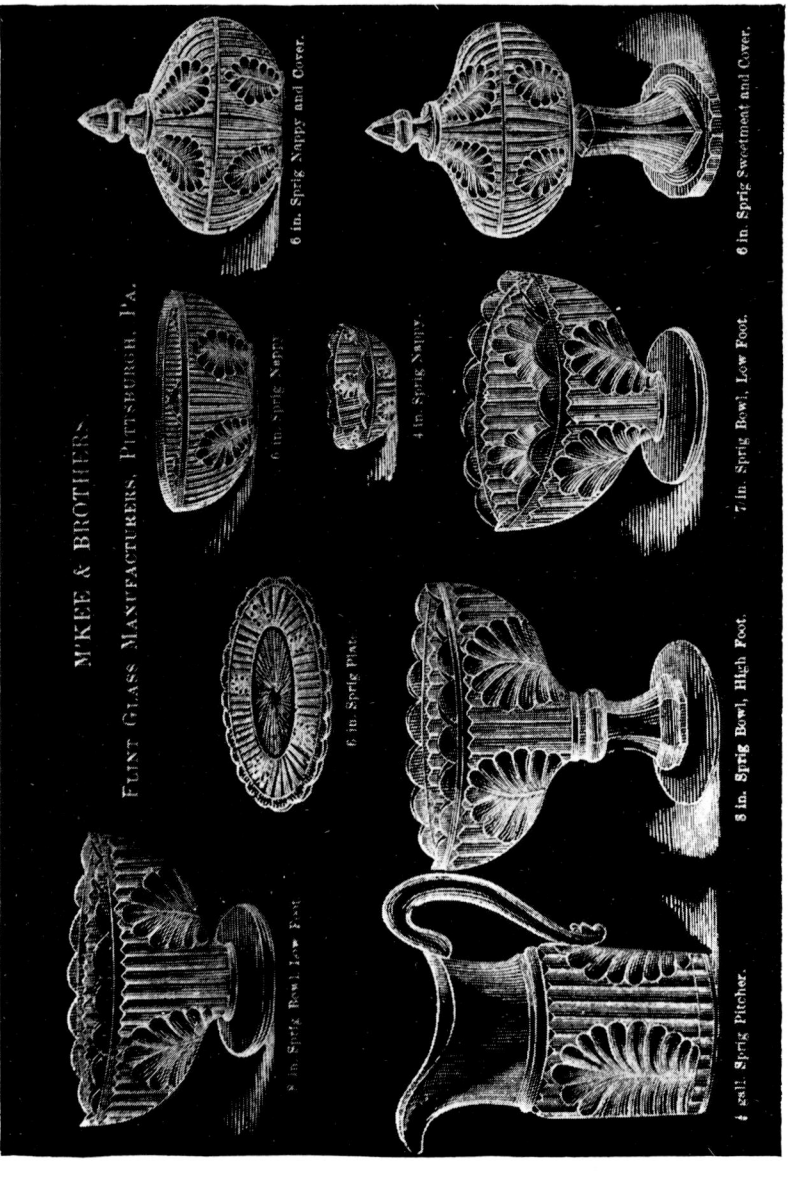

PLATE 38

Group of Ribbed Palm, originally termed "Sprig," as shown by M'Kee & Brothers of Pittsburgh, Pa., in the 1860's.

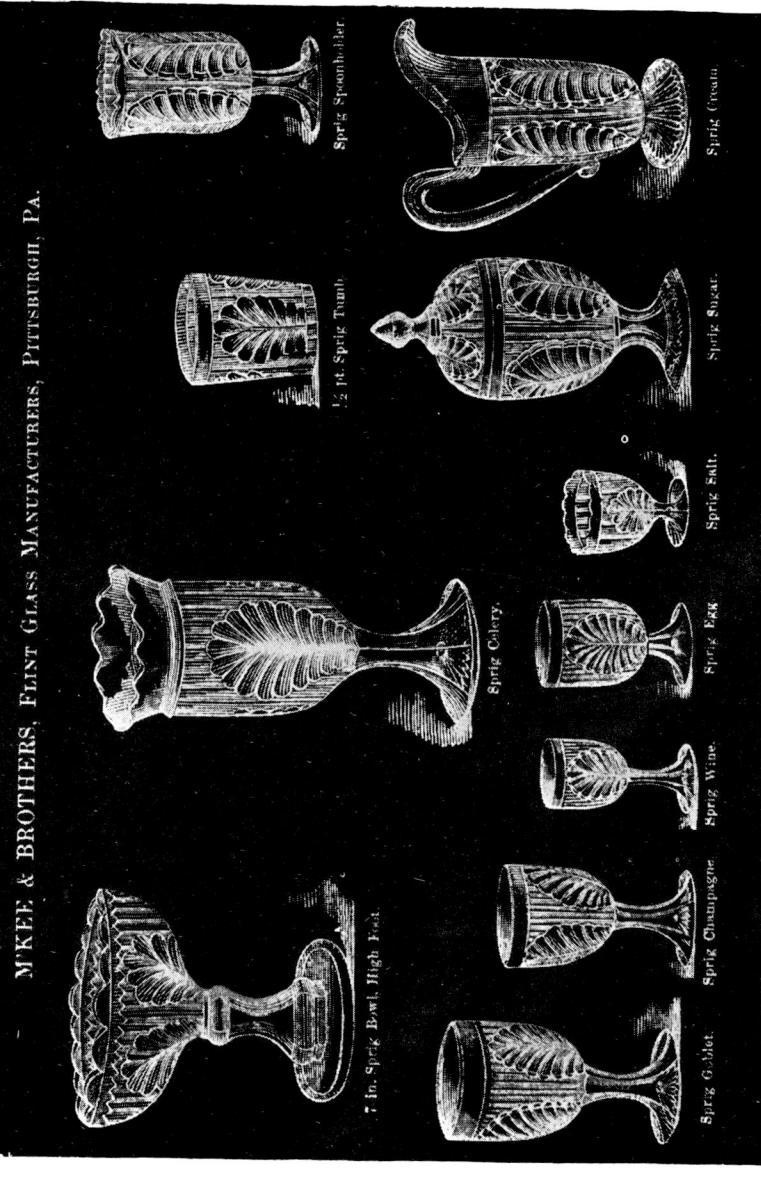

PLATE 38A

Group of Ribbed Palm, originally termed "Sprig," as shown by M'Kee & Brothers of Pittsburgh, Pa., in the 1860's.

PLATE 39
1. RIBBED ACORN butter dish, compote, sweetmeat.
2. Bowl of RIBBED ACORN compote and sauce dish.
3. RIBBED IVY creamer, sugar bowl, spoonholder.
4. RIBBED IVY whiskey tumbler, butter dish, covered salt.

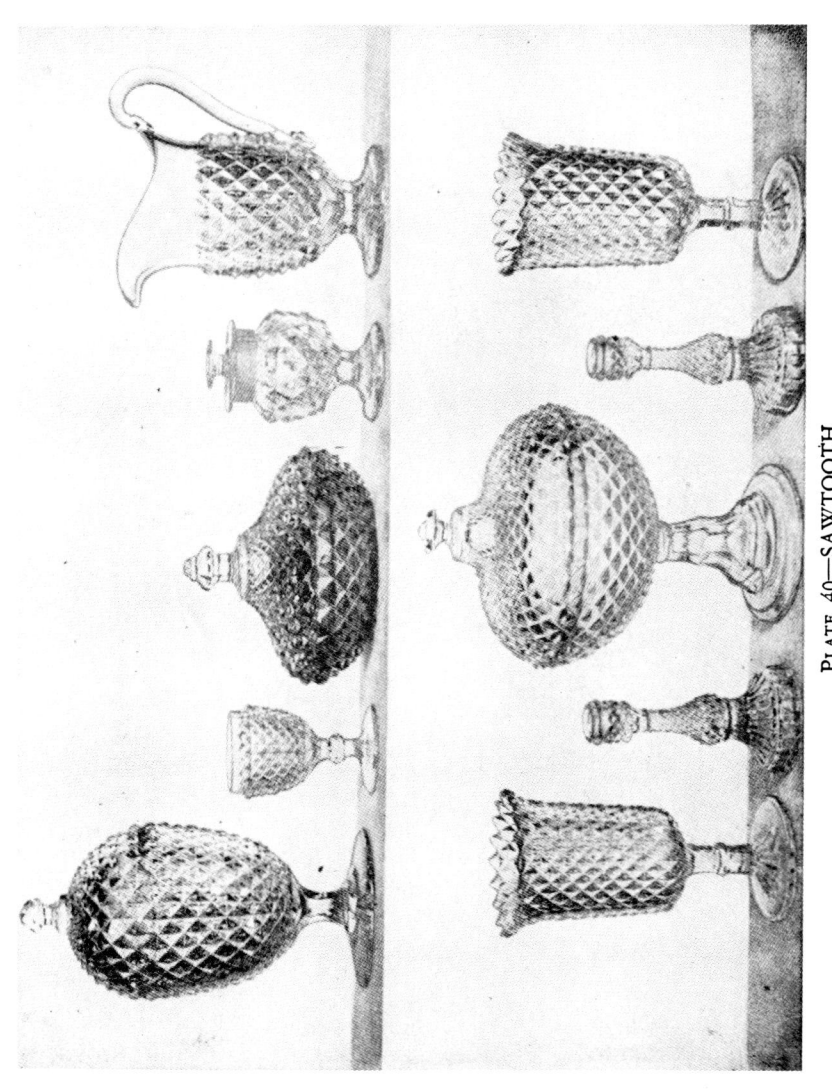

PLATE 40—SAWTOOTH
Sugar bowl   Wine glass   Butter dish   Pomade jar   Creamer
Pair of celery vases   Pair of candlesticks   Compote on high foot

PLATE 41—SAWTOOTH OF LATER PERIOD

Pair of covered dishes with lion handles and knobs Open compote in center
Sugar bowl   Cake plate on standard   Creamer

PLATE 42—GOBLETS

New England Pineapple
Sawtooth

Tulip
Diamond Point

PLATE 43—GROUP OF DIAMOND POINT

Celery vase Egg cup Open compote Tumbler Water pitcher
Lamp Covered salt Pint decanter Handled mug Quart decanter

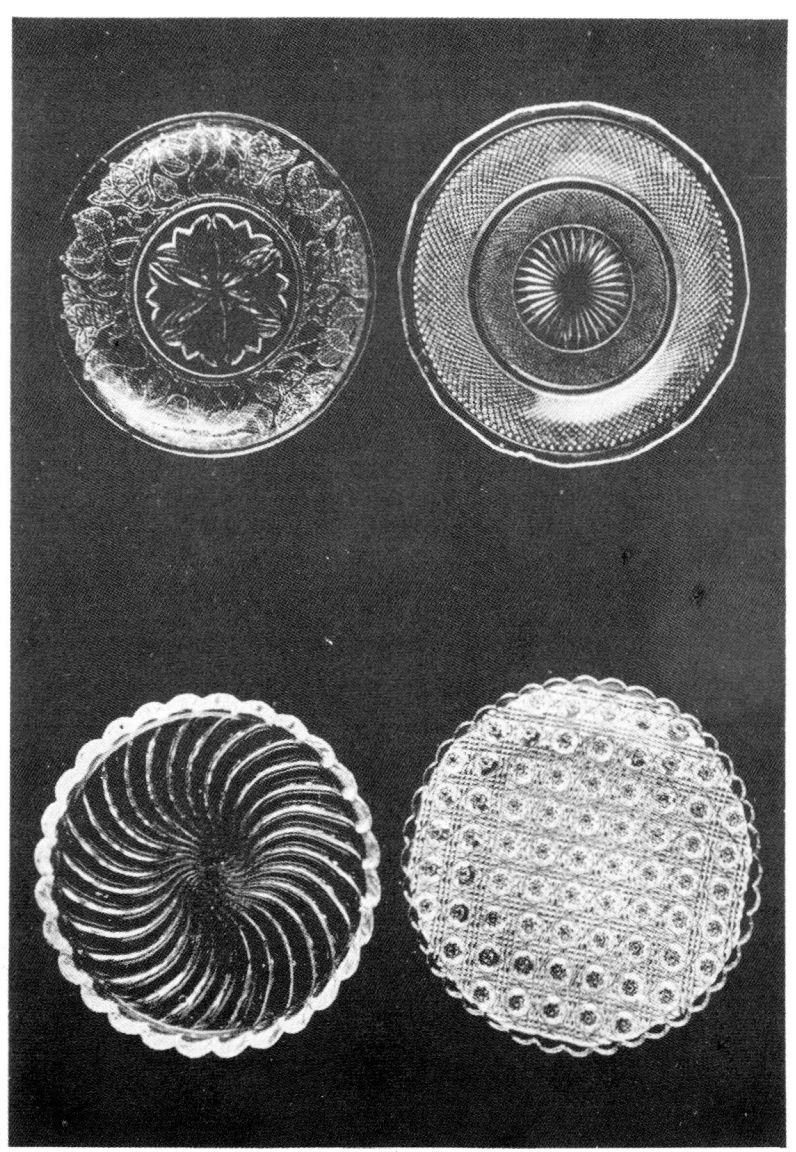

PLATE 44—PLATES

Beaded Tulip
Pinwheel

Diamond Point
Daisy

PLATE 45—PLATES

Diamond Point, star and circle center Diamond Point, star center
Willow Oak Single Tulip

PLATE 46
1. WAFFLE celery vase, water tumbler, butter dish, egg cup.
2. LINCOLN DRAPE compote, syrup pitcher, spoonholder, butter dish.
3. LINCOLN DRAPE compote, sauce dish, footed salt, egg cup.
4. LINCOLN DRAPE with TASSEL goblet, compote, spoonholder.

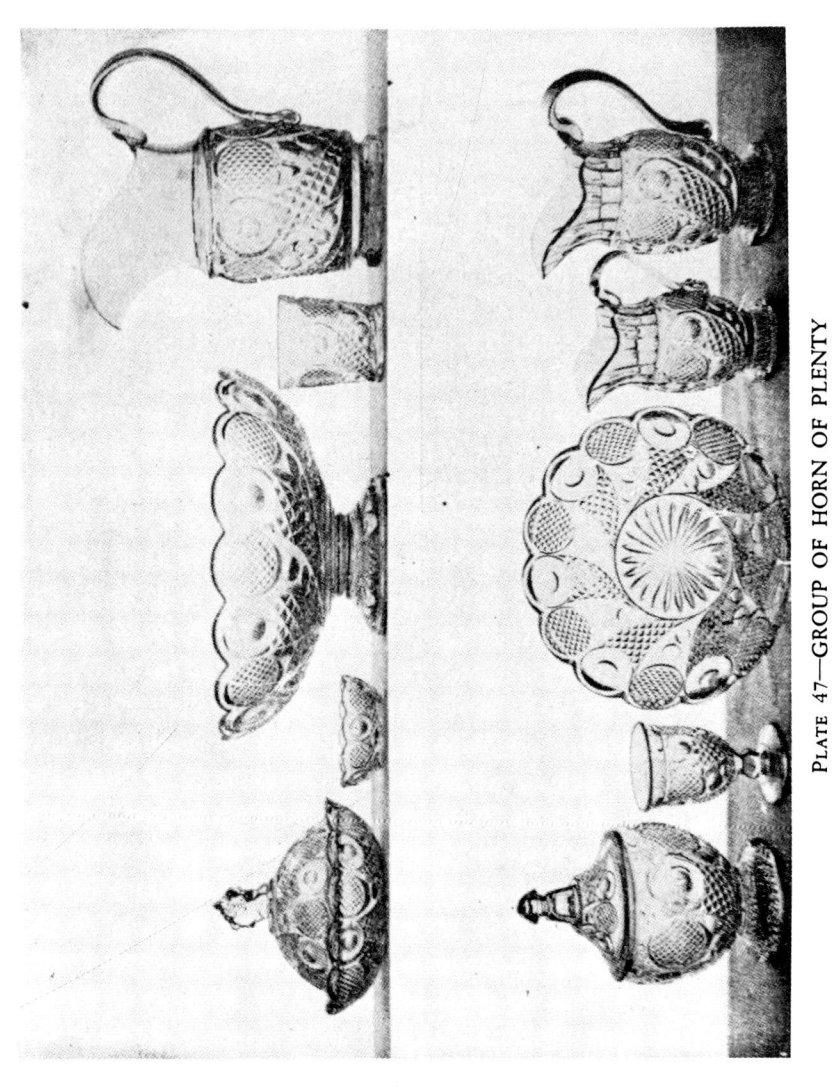

PLATE 47—GROUP OF HORN OF PLENTY

Rare butter dish with knob in form of Washington's head, oval salt, compote, tumbler, water pitcher. Sugar bowl, egg cup, bowl, creamers in two sizes

PLATE 48—GOBLETS

Bull's Eye with Fleur de Lys
Comet

Bull's Eye
Horn of Plenty

PLATE 49

1. BULL'S EYE goblet with knob stem; goblet, plainer stem; cordial; egg cup; salt.
2. BULL'S EYE pickle dish, sugar bowl, tumbler.
3. COMET goblet, water pitcher, whiskey tumbler.
4. BULL'S EYE with DIAMOND POINT celery vase, cruet, egg cup, sauce dish.

PLATE 50
1. TULIP VARIANTS (later period) sugar bowl, goblet, cordial, celery variant without sawtooth at base of petals.
2. BULL'S EYE VARIANT goblet, footed tumbler, water tumbler, castor bottle.
3. JACOB'S LADDER creamer, jam jar, plate, cordial.
4 WHEAT and BARLEY mug, celery vase, water pitcher, footed sauce dish.

PLATE 51—BULL'S EYE WITH FLEUR DE LYS

Water pitcher   Goblet   Sugar bowl   Lamp

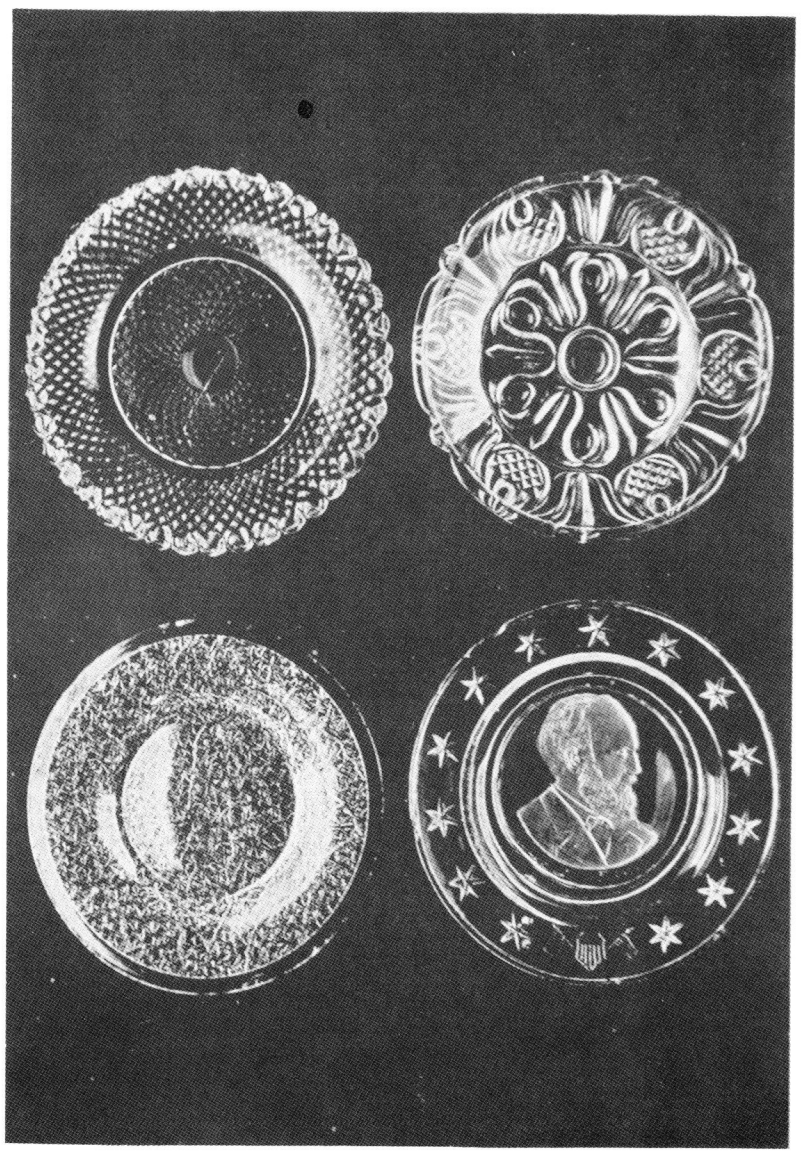

PLATE 52—SIX INCH PLATES
Diamond Quilted with Bull's Eye border   New England Pineapple
Tree of Life   Garfield

PLATE 53
1. TULIP butter dish, creamer, pomade jar.
2. TULIP celery vase, quart decanter with original patent stopper (Tulip stopper in insert), cordial, footed salt.
3. NEW ENGLAND PINEAPPLE open compote on high foot, creamer, sugar bowl.
4. NEW ENGLAND PINEAPPLE tumbler, sauce dish, egg cup.

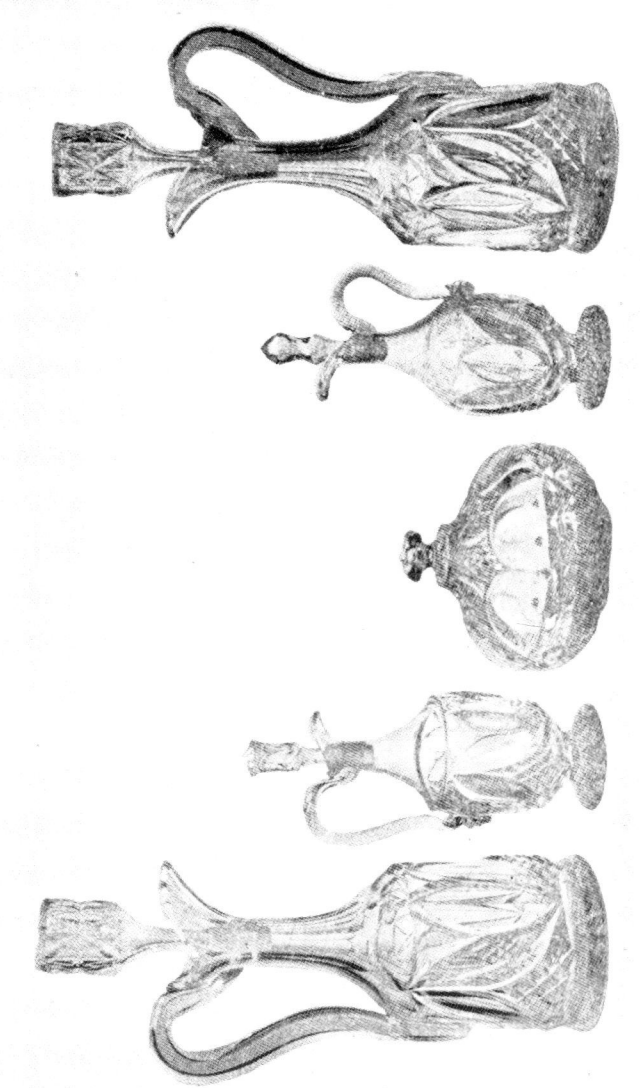

PLATE 54—TULIP
Pair of large jugs, pair of small cruets and butter dish.

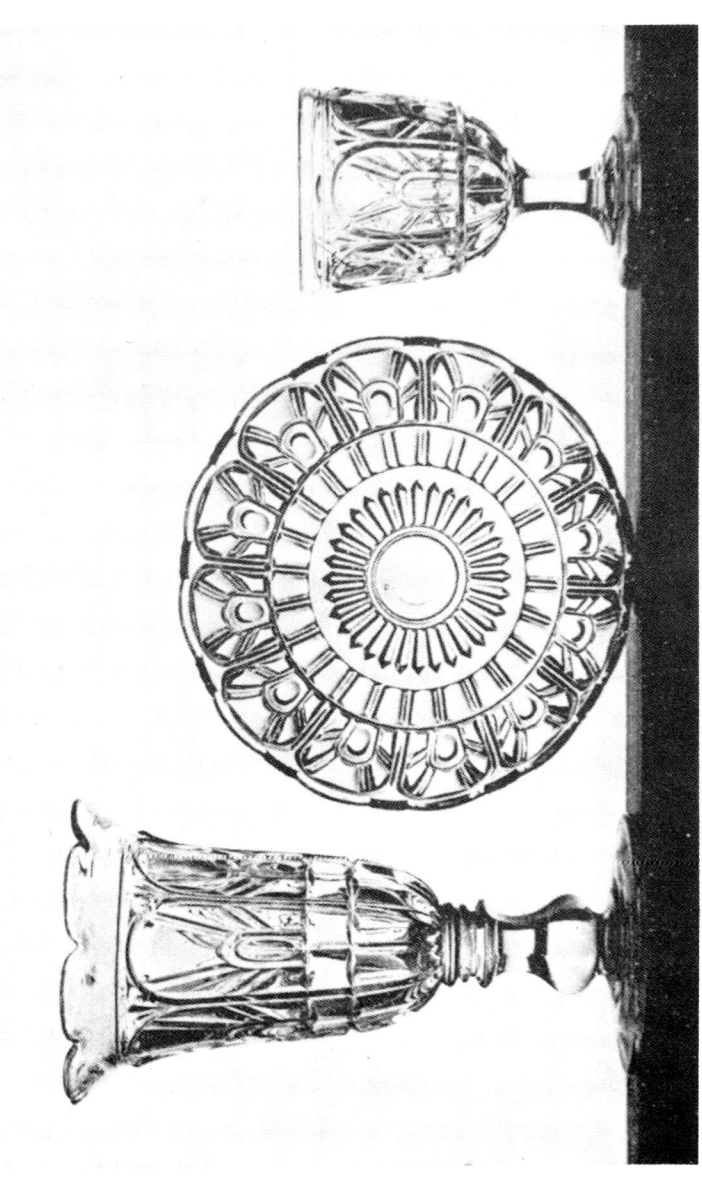

Celery vase　　Plate 55—GOTHIC　　Goblet
　　　　　　　　　　Bowl

PLATE 56—HAMILTON

Egg cup　Tumbler　　　　　Compote　Creamer　Butter dish　Spoonholder
　　Sugar bowl　　　　　　　　Water-pitcher　Goblet

PLATE 57—GOBLETS

Dew with Raindrop Beaded dewdrop
Hamilton with Leaf Jacob's Ladder

PLATE 58
1. CATHEDRAL sugar bowl, spoonholder, footed sauce dish, cordial.
2. LIBERTY BELL creamer, spoonholder, goblet, butter dish.
3. ANTHEMION plate with rolled edges, tumbler, sauce dish.
4. CABLE with RING sugar bowl, creamer, bowl of sauce dish.

PLATE 59—THUMBPRINT

Pair of covered compotes Large open compote Covered compote
Small open compote Cordial Decanter Tumbler Goblet

PLATE 60
1. HONEYCOMB handled egg cup, finger bowl, salt.
   Known as "New York" pattern by M'Kee Bros., of Pittsburgh and by the New England Glass Co.
2. HONEYCOMB compote on high foot, compote on low foot, celery vase.
3. HONEYCOMB sugar bowl, creamer, two styles of egg cups.
   Known as "Cincinnati" by M'Kee Bros., and as "Vernon" at the New England Glass Co.
4. HONEYCOMB decanter, covered salt, open salt, shakers.

PLATE 61
1. FINE CUT and PANEL sugar bowl, compote, footed sauce dish.
2. BAND sugar bowl, footed tumbler, goblet.
3. PHILADELPHIA compote on low foot, footed sauce, smaller compote.
4. BEADED BAND goblet, cordial, water pitcher.

PLATE 62—GOBLETS

Magnet and Grape
Banded Buckle

Oval Panel
Buckle

PLATE 63
1. BEADED GRAPE celery vase, tumbler, butter dish, creamer.
2. MAGNET and GRAPE (frosted leaf) goblet, tumbler, creamer, salt.
3. GRAPE and FESTOON goblet (stippled leaf), butter dish, creamer, goblet (clear leaf).
4. STIPPLED GRAPE and FESTOON celery vase, creamer, goblets (clear and stippled leaf).

PLATE 64
1. PANELLED GRAPE celery vase, spoonholder, water pitcher.
2. PANELLED GRAPE sugar bowl, creamer, goblet.
3. ARCHED GRAPE goblet, spoonholder, creamer, butter dish.
4. GRAPE BAND goblet, creamer, spoonholder, cordial.

PLATE 65
1. LATE PANELLED GRAPE goblet, covered bowl, butter dish.
2. FLATTENED SAWTOOTH compote, footed salt, water pitcher.
3. BEADED ACORN goblet, spoonholder, footed salt, egg cup.
4. CABBAGE LEAF bowl of sauce dish, celery vase, butter dish.

PLATE 66
1. BALTIMORE PEAR sugar bowl, water pitcher, spoonholder.
2. CHERRY goblet, sugar bowl, sauce dish.
3. BEADED GRAPE MEDALLION (banded) covered compote, pickle dish, creamer.
4. BEADED GRAPE MEDALLION goblets and their different bases.

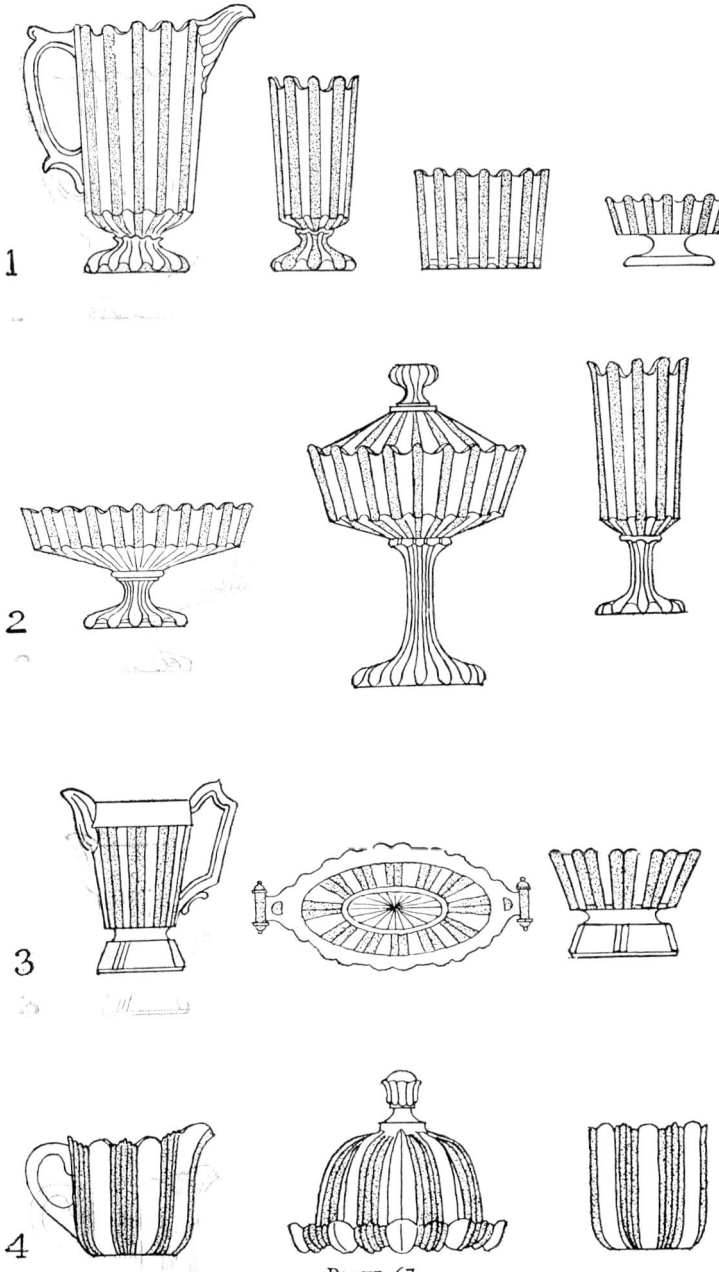

PLATE 67
1. RIBBON water pitcher, spoonholder, bowl, footed sauce dish.
2. RIBBON compote on low foot, compote on high standard, celery vase.
3. DOUBLE RIBBON creamer, pickle dish, footed sauce dish.
4. FLUTED RIBBON creamer, butter dish, spoonholder.

PLATE 68

Pair of relish dishes with frosted centers, showing mountains and a St. Bernard dog. Plate in Frosted Stork, Dolphin dish with bowl in Ribbon pattern. Ribbon goblet.

PLATE 69
1. FROSTED RIBBON celery vase, goblet, footed sauce dish.
2. DEW and RAINDROP berry bowl, tumbler, sauce dish.
3. SWIRL celery vase, butter dish, tumbler.
4. MOON and STAR berry bowl, sugar bowl, butter dish.

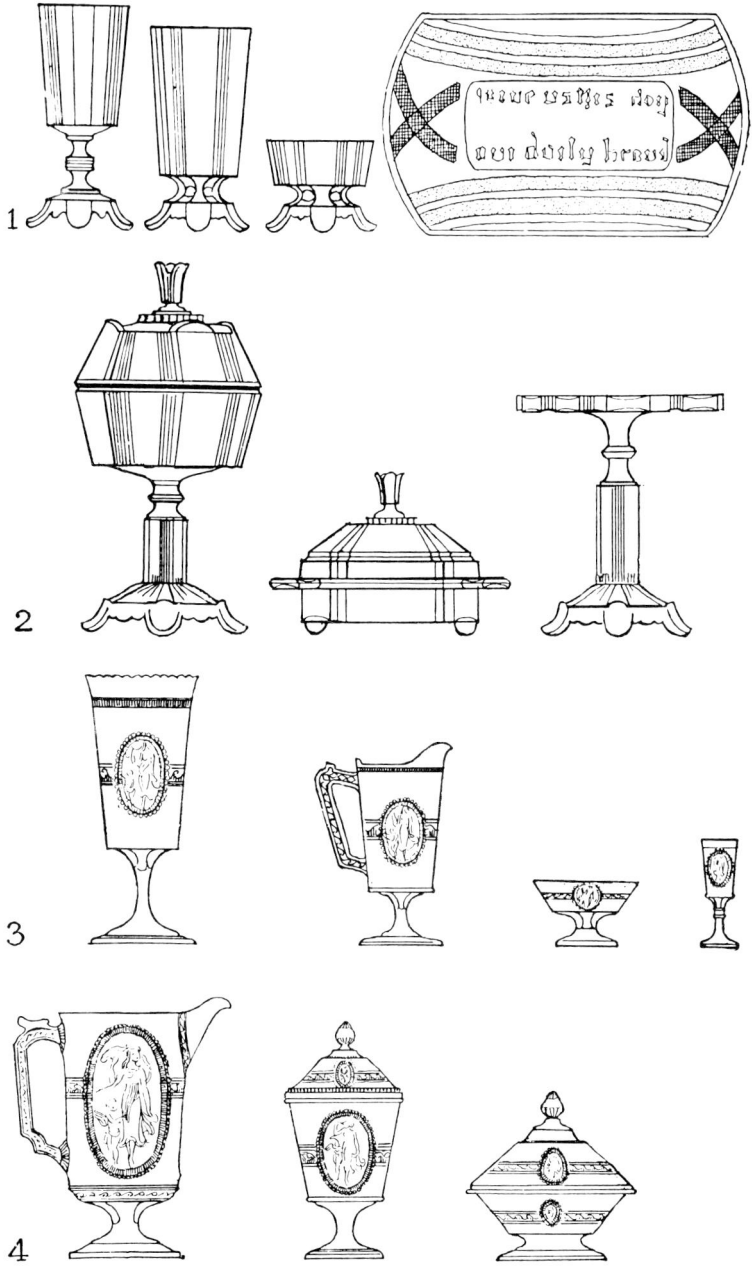

PLATE 70
1. CLEAR RIBBON goblet, spoonholder, sauce dish, bread tray.
2. CLEAR RIBBON compote, butter dish, cake plate on standard.
3. CUPID and VENUS celery vase, creamer, footed sauce dish, cordial.
4. CUPID and VENUS water pitcher, sugar bowl, butter dish.

PLATE 71—GOBLETS

Hobnail with Fan top   Flattened Hobnail
Dewdrop   Popcorn

PLATE 72—GOBLETS

"101" Panelled Dewdrop
Printed Hobnail Late Buckle

PLATE 73—LARGE PLATES

Rose in Snow
Dewdrop with Sheaf of Wheat
Dewdrop with Star
Arched Leaf

PLATE 74—SEVEN INCH PLATES

Stippled Forget-me-not
Hobnail

Snakeskin with Dot, three sizes
"101"

PLATE 75
1. PSYCHE and CUPID sugar bowl, goblet, celery vase.
2. CLEMATIS goblet, spoonholder, sauce dish.
3. JEWEL with DEWDROP pitcher, sauce dish, cordial.
4. PANELLED DEWDROP celery vase, lemonade, goblet.

PLATE 76
1. FROSTED CIRCLE spoonholder, compote on high standard, butter dish.
2. BEADED LOOP sugar bowl, bowl (cover missing), goblet.
3. FAN with DIAMOND sugar bowl, creamer, spoonholder.
4. PLAID sugar bowl (cover missing), pickle dish, celery vase.

PLATE 77
1. BEADED OVAL and SCROLL goblet, creamer, sauce dish.
2. PANELLED FLOWER STIPPLED spoonholder, oval dish, sugar bowl.
3. SWAN creamer, oval covered dish, goblet.
4. FORGET-ME-NOT and SCROLL creamer, sugar bowl, spoonholder.

PLATE 78
1. LATTICE sugar bowl, butter dish, goblet.
2. SPRIG goblet, open compote, sauce dish.
3. TEARDROP and TASSEL compote, water pitcher, sauce dish.
4. DIAMOND SUNBURST water pitcher, goblet, sauce dish.

PLATE 79
1. PANELLED FORGET-ME-NOT goblet, butter dish, bowl (cover missing).
2. LOOP with DEWDROPS goblet, cordial, sugar bowl, creamer.
3. POWDER and SHOT goblet, creamer, sugar bowl, butter dish.
4. PANELLED CHERRY goblet, butter dish, rare hat made from goblet mold.

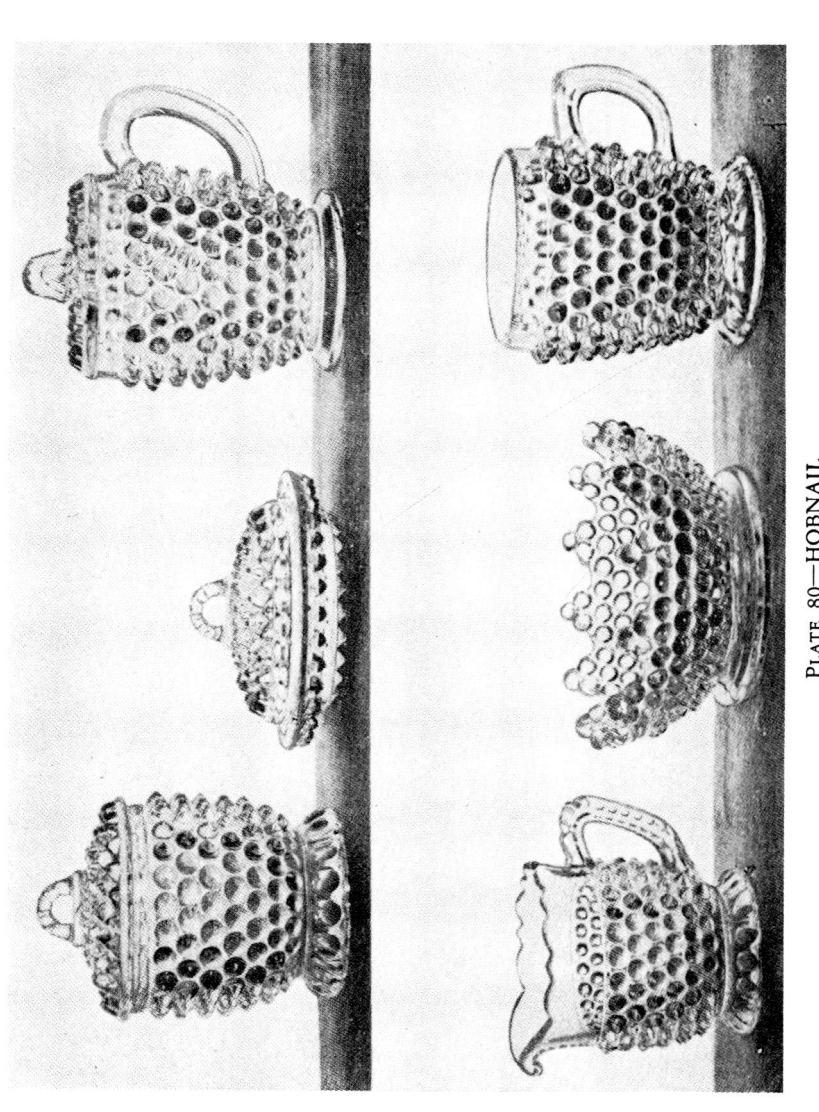

PLATE 80—HOBNAIL
Mustard jar (Thumbprint base), butter dish of child's set, mustard jar with handle
Creamer (Thumbprint base), sauce dish, mug (Thumbprint base)

PLATE 81—HOBNAIL

Creamer Butter dish Spoonholder (Ball feet)
Finger bowl (Thumbprint base) Goblet Open sugar (Ball feet)

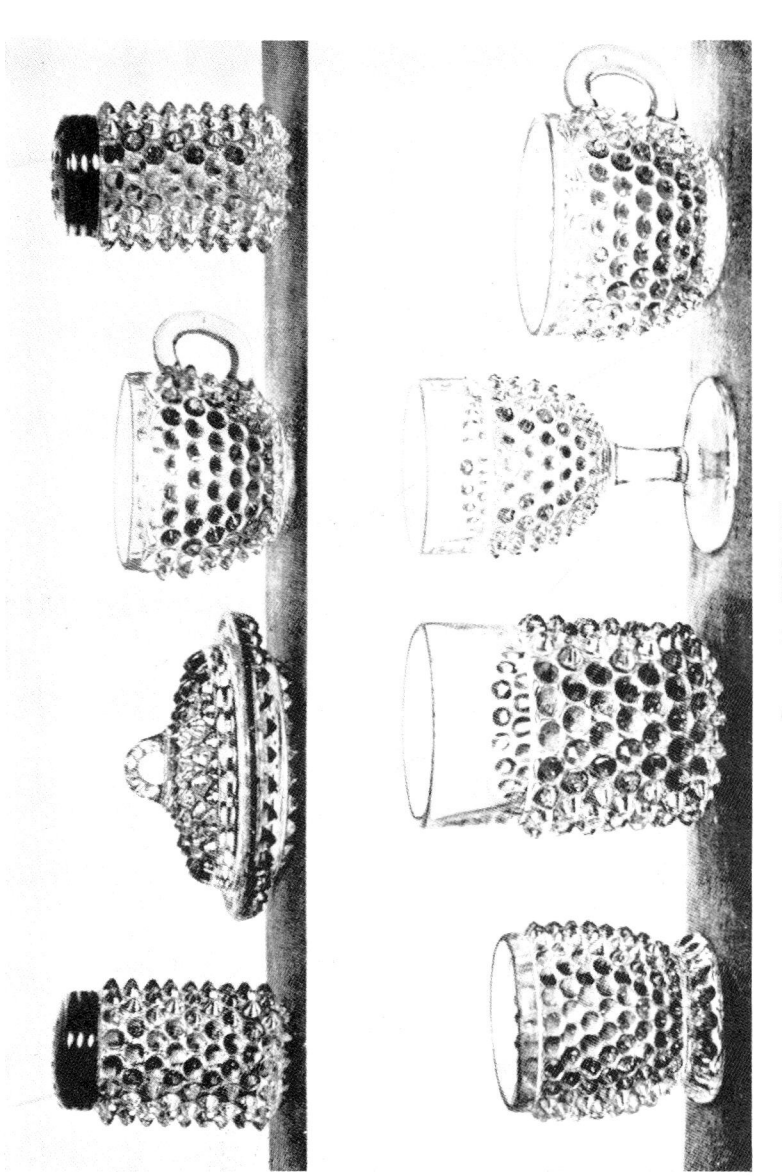

PLATE 82—HOBNAIL

Salt and pepper shakers   Butter dish of child's set   Sherbet Cup
Sugar bowl of child's set   Tumbler   Cordial   Cup showing ornamented band

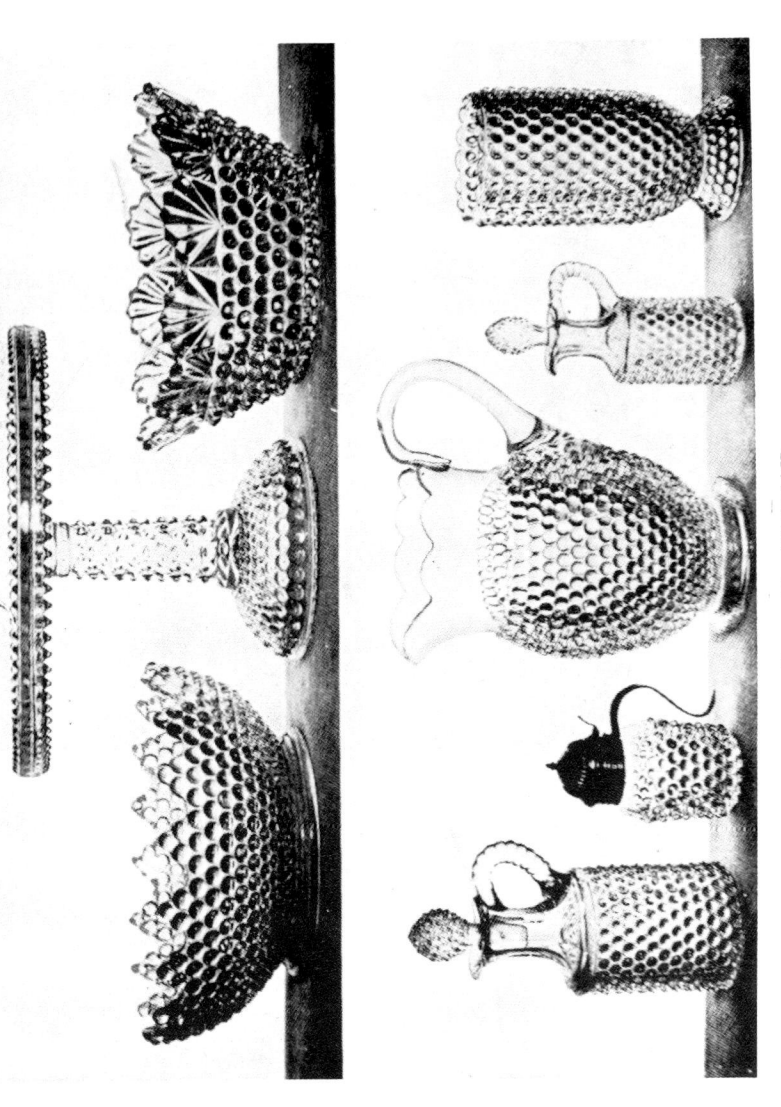

PLATE 83—HOBNAIL

Berry bowl with pointed edge   Cake plate on standard   Berry bowl with fan top
Cruets in two sizes   Mustard jar   Water pitcher   Celery vase

PLATE 84
1. OPAL HOBNAIL (frilled top) celery vase, creamer, tumbler.
2. OPAL HOBNAIL (three feet) celery vase, creamer, tumbler.
3. OPAL HOBNAIL (four feet) sugar bowl, creamer, butter dish.
4. PANELED HOBNAIL compote, berry bowl.

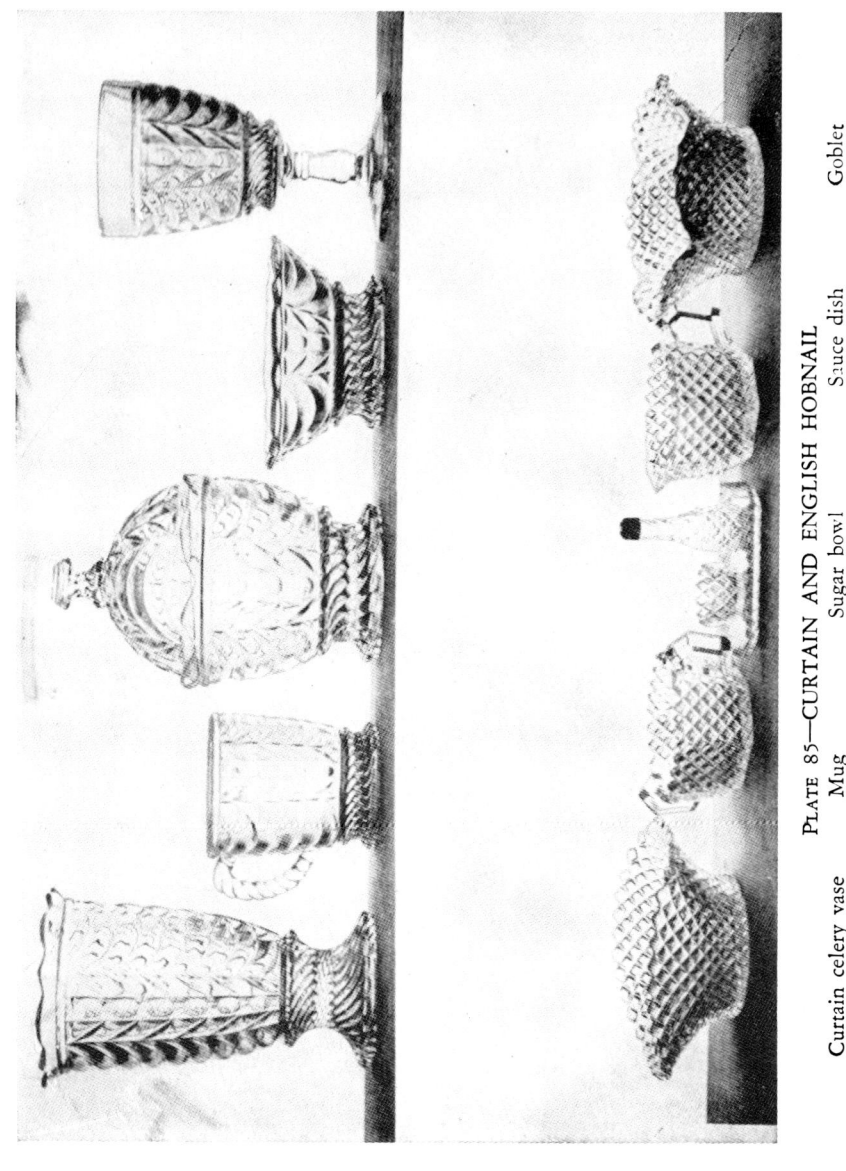

PLATE 85—CURTAIN AND ENGLISH HOBNAIL

Curtain celery vase   Mug   Sugar bowl   Sauce dish   Goblet
English Hobnail bowl   Sugar and creamer   Salt and pepper on tray   Bowl

PLATE 86—GOBLETS

Paneled Diamond Point
Forget-Me-Not in Scroll

English Hobnail, Paneled
Rose Sprig

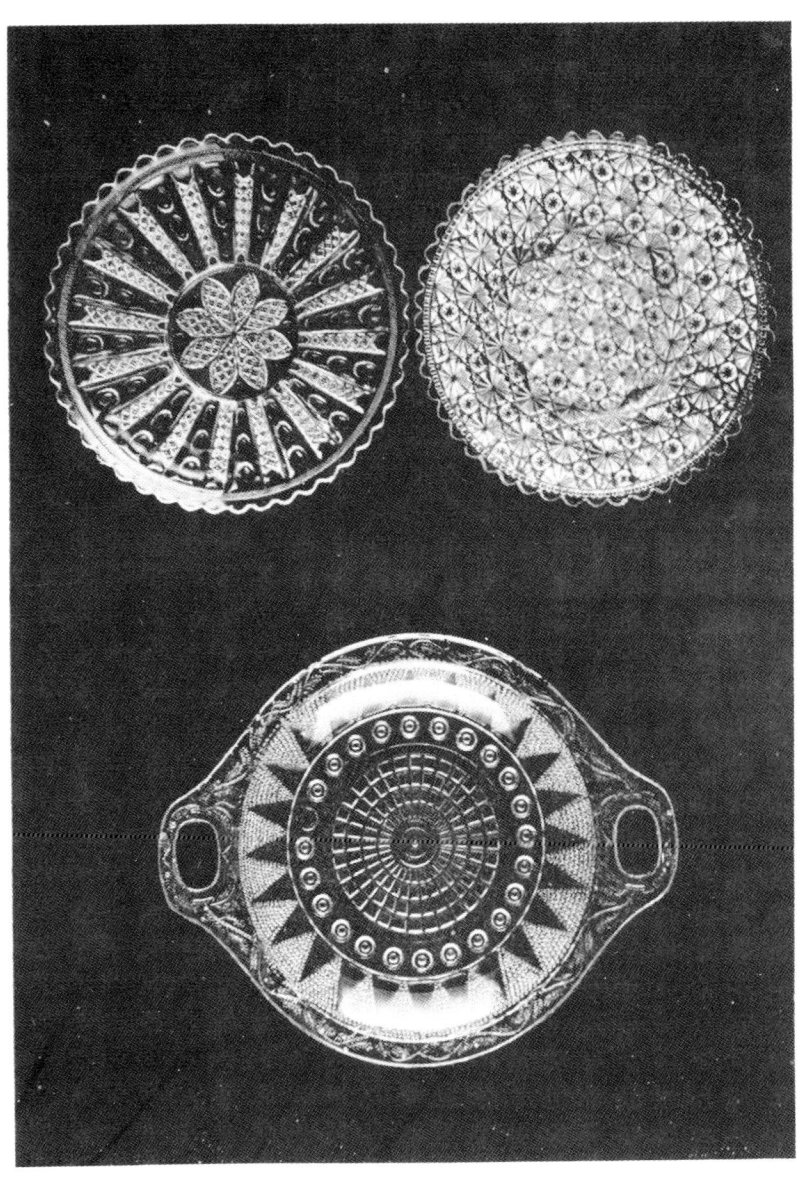

PLATE 87—LARGE PLATES
English Hobnail and Thumbprint Daisy and Burton
Dewdrop in Points, vine border

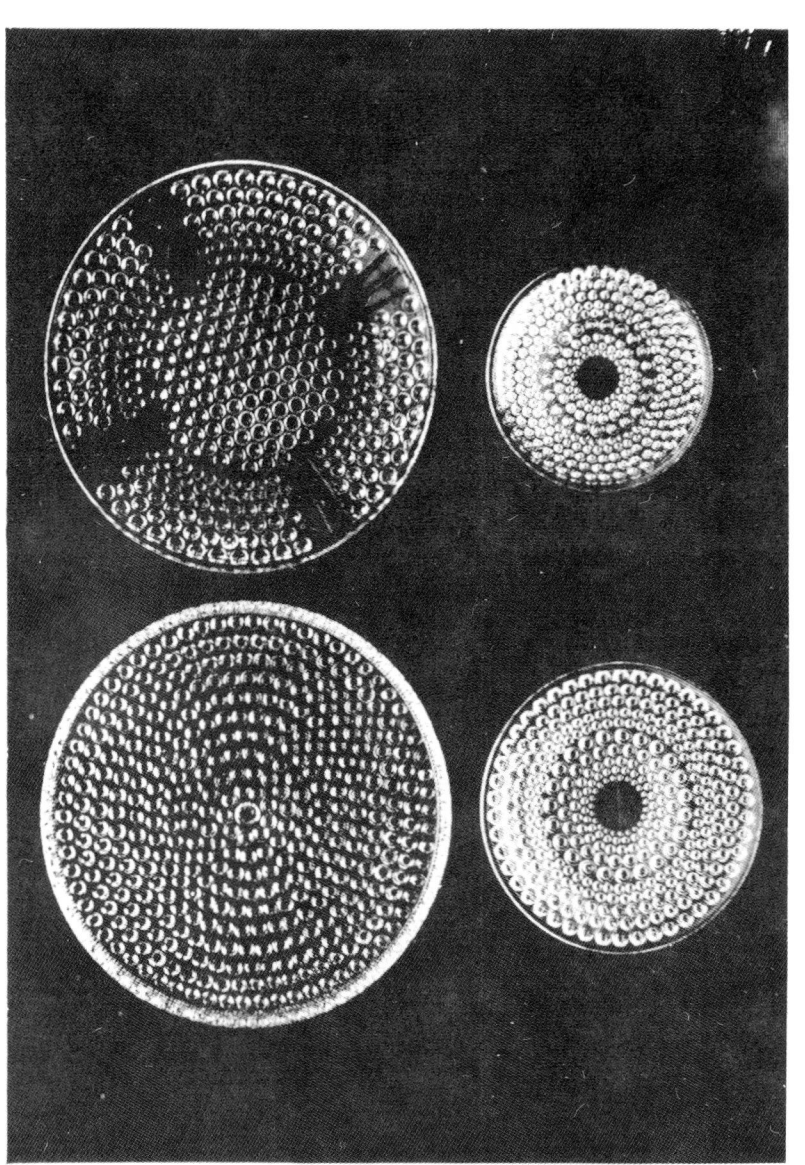

PLATE 88—HOBNAIL.
Tray for water set   Plate in Paneled Hobnail
Saucers for cups, illustrated on Plate 82

PLATE 89
1. WESTWARD-HO compote. sugar bowl, creamer, marmalade jar.
2. WESTWARD-HO butter dish, celery vase, footed sauce dish.
3. THREE-FACE compote, salt shaker, sugar bowl, butter dish.
4. BABY-FACE sugar bowl, spoonholder, goblet.

PLATE 90

Lion lamp, clear glass with frosted heads. It is 7¾ inches high to the top of the collar and 5 inches across the widest part of the bowl.

PLATE 91—GOBLETS

Lion
Polar Bear

Three-Face
Westward-Ho

PLATE 92—PLATES AND PLATTERS

Lion platter — Lion bread plate
Westward-Ho platter — Cupid and Venus bread plate

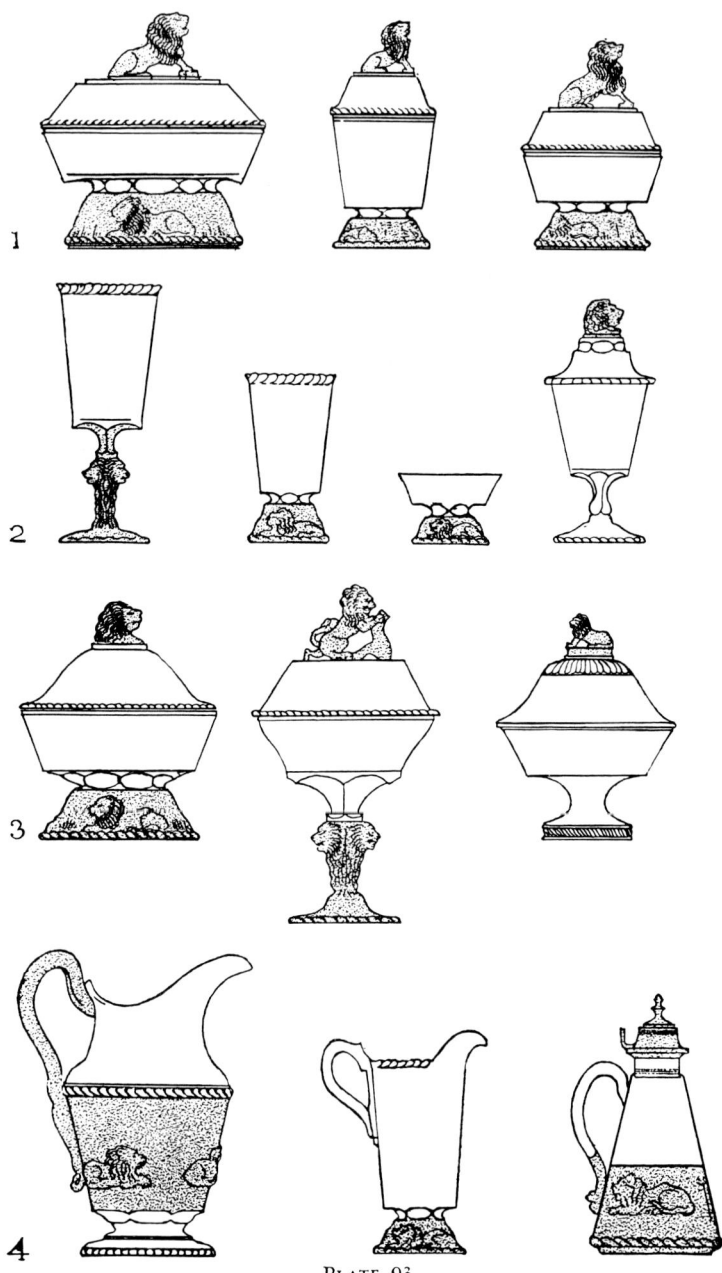

PLATE 93

1. LION oblong covered dish, sugar bowl, butter dish.
2. LION celery vase, spoonholder, footed sauce, sugar bowl.
3. LION covered dish, compote on high standard, compote on low foot.
4. LION water pitcher, creamer, syrup pitcher.

PLATE 94
1. JUMBO spoon rack, covered compote.
2. POLAR BEAR clear goblet, goblet frosted and clear, bowl.
3. FROSTED LEAF footed tumbler, decanter, goblet.
4. ROMAN KEY goblet, open compote on high standard, sauce dish.

Collection of Dr. Charles Ferris.

PLATE 94A
Upper: Monkey tumbler, waste bowl, spoonholder.
Lower: Butter dish, showing rayed base; pickle jar.

PLATE 95—CELERY VASES
Palmette
Roman Key (English type)
Paneled Daisy
Leaf and Dart

PLATE 96—GOBLETS

Three Panel Frosted Circle
Teasel Prism with Diamond Points

PLATE 97—CLASSIC—SHELL AND TASSEL
Classic spoonholder   Butter dish   Sugar bowl (cover missing)   Creamer
Shell and Tassel pair of celery vases   Goblet   Water pitcher

PLATE 98—GOBLETS

Garfield Drape Cardinal Bird
Star Rosetted Classic

PLATE 99—COVERED DISHES

Pair of compotes with frosted eagle knobs
Compote with knob in form of large dog, frosted

Pair of oval dishes with knobs in form of pheasants, frosted
Frosted Stork sugar bowl

PLATE 100

1. CARDINAL BIRD sugar bowl, creamer, spoonholder, footed sauce dish.
2. OWL and POSSUM goblet, showing both sides of bowl, PARROT goblet.
3. FROSTED STORK sugar bowl, goblet, spoonholder.
4. SQUIRREL goblet, water pitcher, footed sauce dish.

PLATE 101
1. DEER and DOG sugar bowl, Dog compote on high standard, Deer and Dog butter dish.
2. DOUBLE LOOP creamer, spoonholder, butter dish.
3. STIPPLED DAISY creamer, spoonholder, oblong dish.
4. BLOCK with THUMBPRINT goblet, footed tumbler, goblet variant.

PLATE 102
1. HONEYCOMB with STAR butter dish, sugar bowl, creamer, spoonholder.
2. MEDALLION water pitcher, butter dish, goblet.
3. BANDED BUCKLE sugar bowl, egg cup, spoonholder.
4. BUCKLE sugar bowl, creamer, egg cup, sauce dish.

PLATE 103—GOBLETS

Moon and Star Gooseberry
Ivy in Snow Diamond Band

PLATE 104
1. DIAMOND QUILTED sugar bowl, celery vase, butter dish, tumbler.
2. GARFIELD DRAPE water pitcher, pickle dish, footed sauce dish.
3. BASKET WEAVE water pitcher, goblet, cup and saucer.
4. PANELLED DIAMOND POINT celery vase, sauce dish, spoonholder.

PLATE 105—PLATTERS

Chain and Shield
Shell and Tassel
Dahlia
Plear and Panel

PLATE 106
1. ROSETTE compote, spoonholder, sugar bowl.
2. LOG CABIN creamer, spoonholder, compote.
3. PEACOCK FEATHER (late) creamer, sauce dish, handled lamp.
4. SHIELD and CHAIN goblet, cordial, sauce dish.

PLATE 107
1. FLOWER BAND compote, footed sauce dish, celery vase.
2. STIPPLED BAND sugar bowl, butter dish, spoonholder.
3. PICKET goblet, celery vase, open compote on high standard.
4. HAND goblet, spoonholder, sugar bowl.

PLATE 108
1. DIAMOND CUT with LEAF creamer, plate, handled cup.
2. SUNFLOWER creamer, spoonholder, butter dish.
3. DRAPERY creamer, spoonholder, sugar bowl.
4. NAILHEAD goblet, butter dish, bowl of sauce dish.

PLATE 109—GOBLETS

Roman Rosette Diamond Cut with Leaf
Princess Feather Flower Band

PLATE 110
Tray in "Currier and Ives" pattern
Railroad Train platter

PLATE 111—GOBLETS

Pleat and Panel Canadian
Cupid and Venus Egyptian

PLATE 112

1. PRINCESS FEATHER sugar bowl, egg cup, water pitcher, covered bowl.
2. PALMETTE creamer, spoonholder, pickle dish, footed salt.
3. CANADIAN jam jar, goblet, cordial, footed sauce dish.
4. HORSESHOE or GOOD LUCK goblet, jam jar, covered bowl, butter dish.

PLATE 113—SIX INCH PLATES

Grape
Liberty Bell

Barley
Canadian

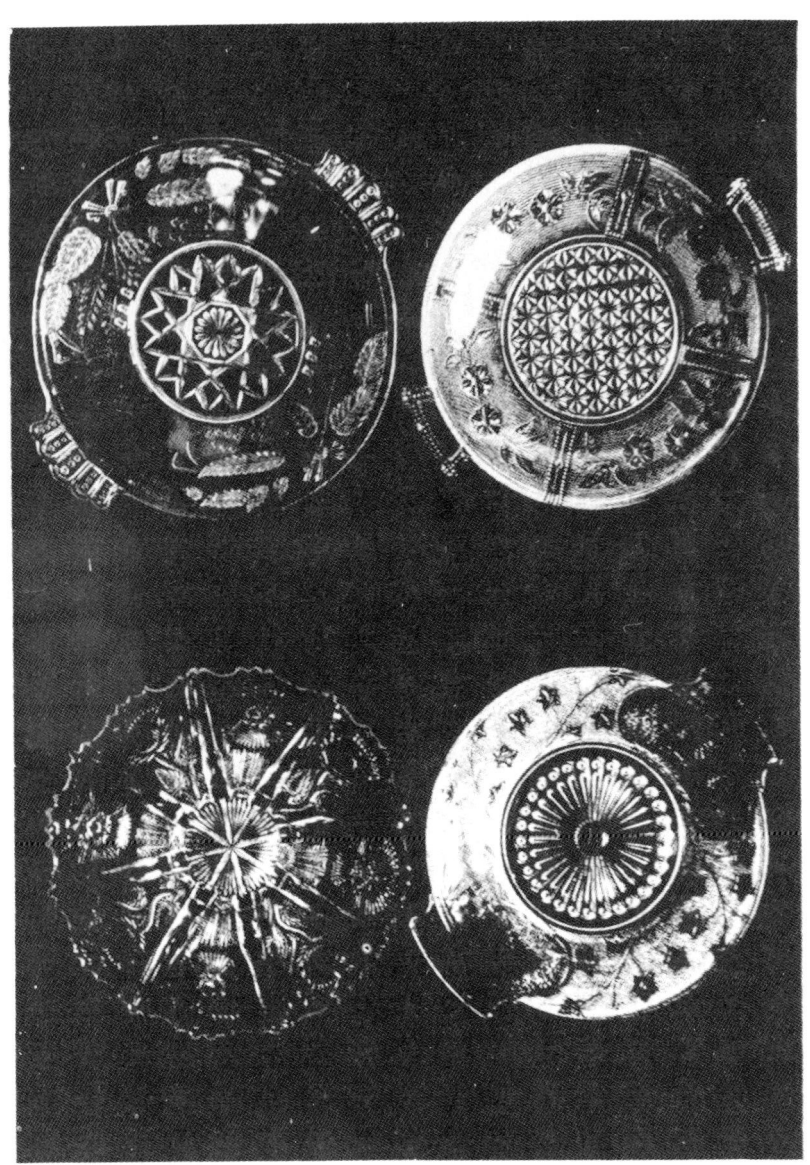

PLATE 114—LARGE PLATES

Wheat and Barley
Paneled Thistle

Primrose
Cape Cod

PLATE 115
1. HERRINGBONE sugar bowl, creamer, butter dish.
2. JACOB'S COAT sugar bowl, creamer, butter dish.
3. MINERVA creamer, spoonholder, footed sauce.
4. CAPE COD sauce dish, goblet, water pitcher, footed sauce.

PLATE 116
1. HOLLY covered compote, goblet, egg cup.
2. CORD and TASSEL wine, celery vase, water pitcher.
3. BARLEY celery vase, jam jar, footed sauce, goblet.
4. BEADED TULIP butter dish, sugar bowl, footed sauce, goblet.

PLATE 117—PLATTERS AND GOBLETS

Liberty Bell Prescott and Stark "The Heroes of Bunker Hill"
Liberty Bell goblet Washington platter Centennial goblet

PLATE 118—BREAD PLATES

Scroll with Flowers
Egyptian

Grape
Centennial, with eagle

PLATE 119

1. DEER and PINE TREE celery vase, butter dish, goblet, footed sauce dish.
2. BUDDED IVY goblet, creamer, spoonholder, butter dish.
3. STIPPLED IVY goblet, sugar bowl, spoonholder, footed salt.
4. IVY in SNOW covered compote, celery vase, cordial, cup and saucer.

PLATE 120—GOBLETS

Rose in snow
Palmette

Fishscale
Windflower

PLATE 121—GOBLETS

Arabesque Minerva
Herringbone Drapery

PLATE 122

1. ROSE in SNOW (square) creamer, sugar bowl, butter dish.
2. ROSE in SNOW (round) sugar bowl, creamer, mug, covered compote on high standard.
3. OPEN ROSE sugar bowl, creamer, egg cup.
4. CABBAGE ROSE goblet, covered compote, cordial.

PLATE 123—GOBLETS

Open Rose
Lily of the Valley

Wildflower
Bleeding Heart

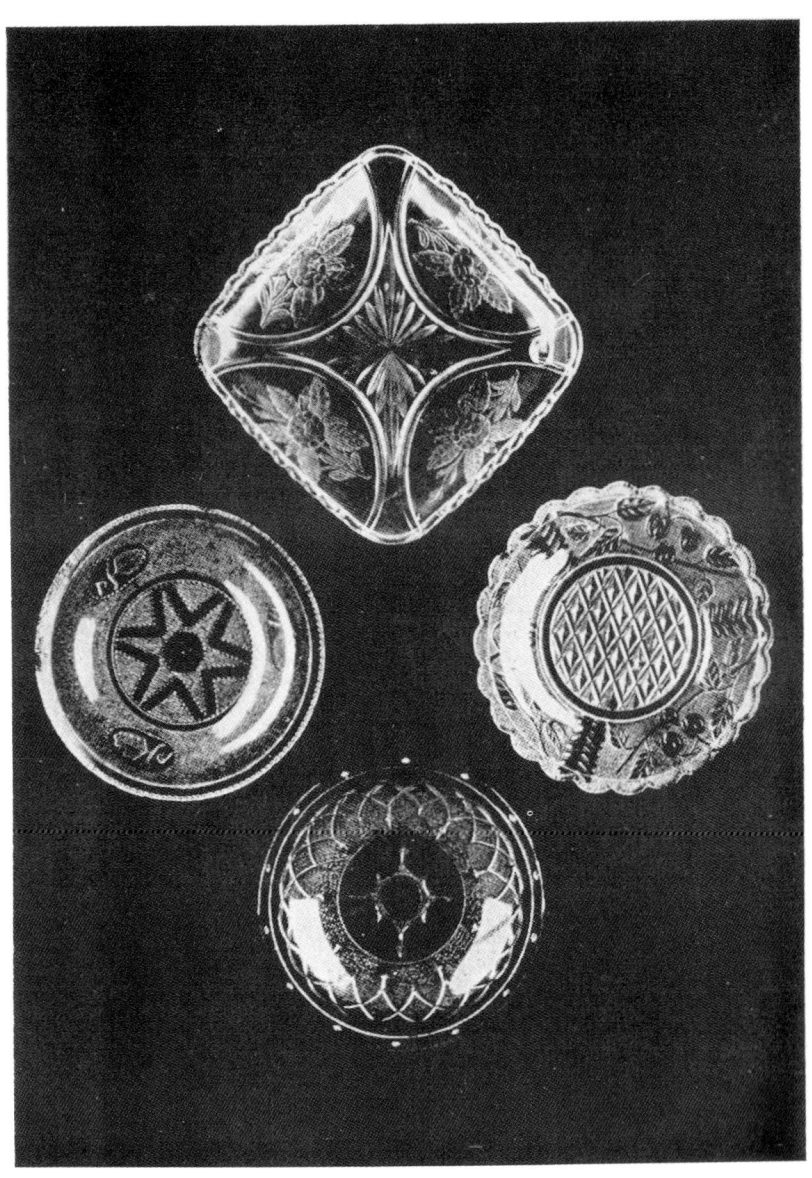

PLATE 124—SIX INCH PLATES
Rose Sprig, Beaded Acorn, Stippled Cherry, Loop and Dart with Diamond Ornaments

PLATE 125
1. ROSE SPRIG water pitcher, relish dish, tumbler.
2. ACORN goblet, butter dish (cover missing), sauce dish.
3. PRESSED LEAF water pitcher, goblet, spoonholder, footed salt.
4. ACORN VARIANTS goblet, goblet with leaf panel, creamer, water pitcher.

PLATE 126

1. DAHLIA creamer, water pitcher, champagne, footed sauce dish.
2. LILY of the VALLEY sugar bowl, goblet, creamer, plain footed creamer.
3. WILDFLOWER water pitcher, creamer, champagne, footed sauce dish.
4. WILDFLOWER celery vase, sugar bowl, tumbler, bowl.

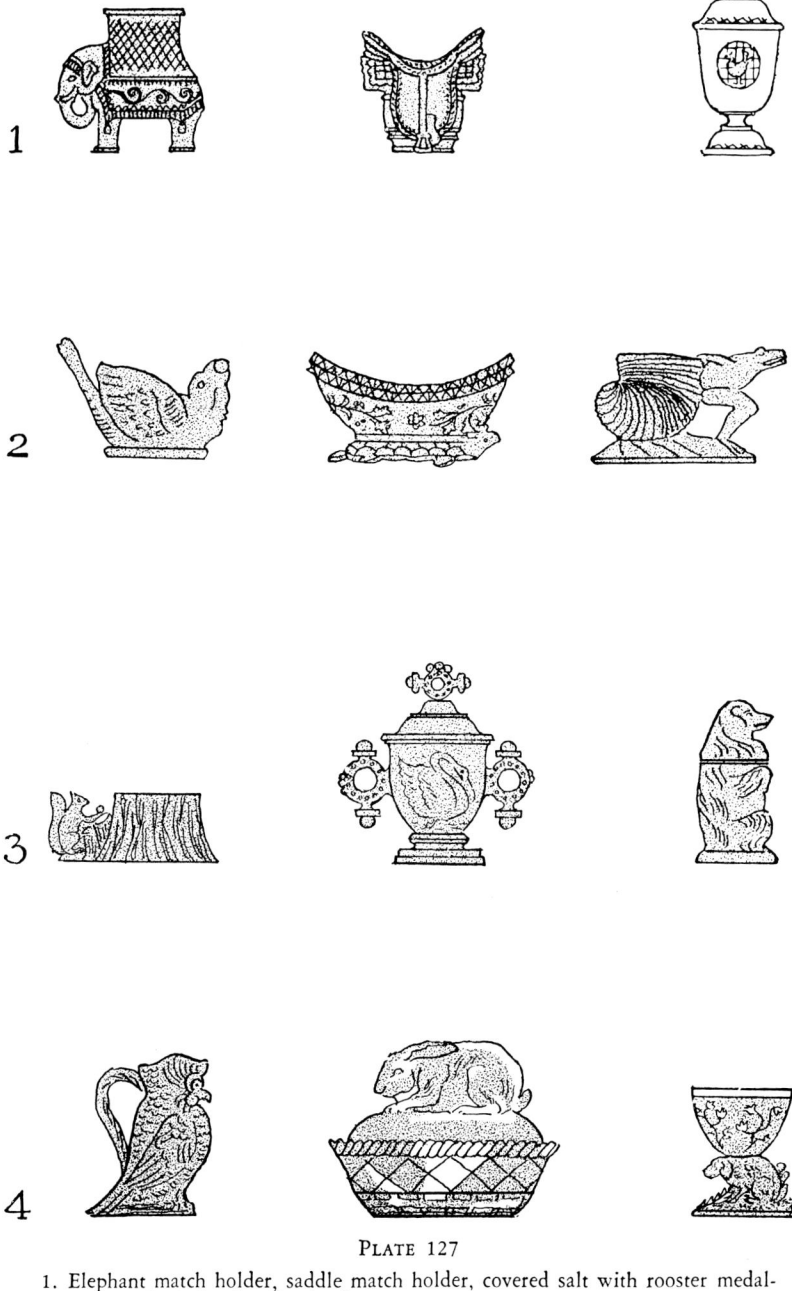

PLATE 127

1. Elephant match holder, saddle match holder, covered salt with rooster medallion, dog's head as knob of cover.
2. Bird salt with cherry in beak, turtle WILDFLOWER salt, frog match holder.
3. Squirrel salt, Swan mustard jar, Bear jar, 4½ inch.
4. Owl creamer, rabbit covered dish, dog salt.

PLATE 128

1. BLEEDING HEART compote on high standard, creamer, butter dish.
2. BLEEDING HEART spoonholder, footed tumbler, tumbler, egg cup.
3. STIPPLED FORGET-ME-NOT cup and saucer, tumbler, oval salt, sauce dish.
4. STIPPLED FORGET-ME-NOT compote on high standard, water pitcher, celery vase.

PLATE 129—LARGE PLATES

Palmette Variant Willow Oak
Dahlia Stippled Forget-Me-Not

PLATE 130—GOBLETS

Stippled Forget-Me-Not
Dahlia

Panelled Forget-Me-Not
Horseshoe or Good Luck

PLATE 131—LARGE PLATES

Horseshoe or Good Luck
Frosted Circle

Star Rosetted
Barred Forget-Me-Not

PLATE 132
1. BARRED FORGET-ME-NOT goblet, pickle dish, cordial.
2. CANE water pitcher, relish dish, spoonholder.
3. DOUBLE SPEAR sugar bowl, creamer, butter dish.
4. CHAIN footed sauce dish, goblet. CHAIN with STAR cordial, plate. 7 inch.

PLATE 133—BREAD PLATES

Horseshoe or Good Luck
Flower Pot

Panelled Forget-Me-Not
The Lord's Supper

PLATE 134—PLATES

Daisy and Button
English Hobnail

Paneled Daisy
Odd seven inch plate

PLATE 135—SIX AND SEVEN INCH PLATES
Princess Feather   Overshot Glass
Barberry   Paneled Daisy
Roman Rosette
Star and Feather

PLATE 136

1. FLOWER POT sugar bowl, creamer, water pitcher.
2. STIPPLED WOODFLOWER sugar bowl, creamer.
3. PRIMROSE covered compote, creamer, goblet, footed sauce.
4. PANELLED DAISY celery vase, compote on high standard, goblet.

PLATE 137
1. RIBBED FORGET-ME-NOT sugar bowl, creamer, butter dish.
2. HEAVY JEWEL sugar bowl, creamer, butter dish, spoonholder.
3. THOUSAND EYE (three knob) celery vase, egg cup, compote.
4. THOUSAND EYE (plain) celery vase, water pitcher, bowl.

PLATE 138—SEVEN-INCH PLATES

Fine Cut Stippled Forget-Me-Not
Diamond Cut with Leaf Dahlia

PLATE 139

1. BARBERRY sugar bowl, pickle dish, spoonholder.
2. BARBERRY covered bowl, covered compote, footed sauce dish.
3. CURRANT sugar bowl, creamer, celery vase.
4. WINDFLOWER creamer, tumbler, spoonholder, egg cup, footed salt.

PLATE 140

1. SCROLL covered compote, sugar bowl, goblet, spoonholder.
2. THISTLE goblet, tumbler, spoonholder, egg cup.
3. SCROLL with FLOWERS creamer, goblet, egg cup.
4. DIAGONAL BAND creamer, goblet, water pitcher.

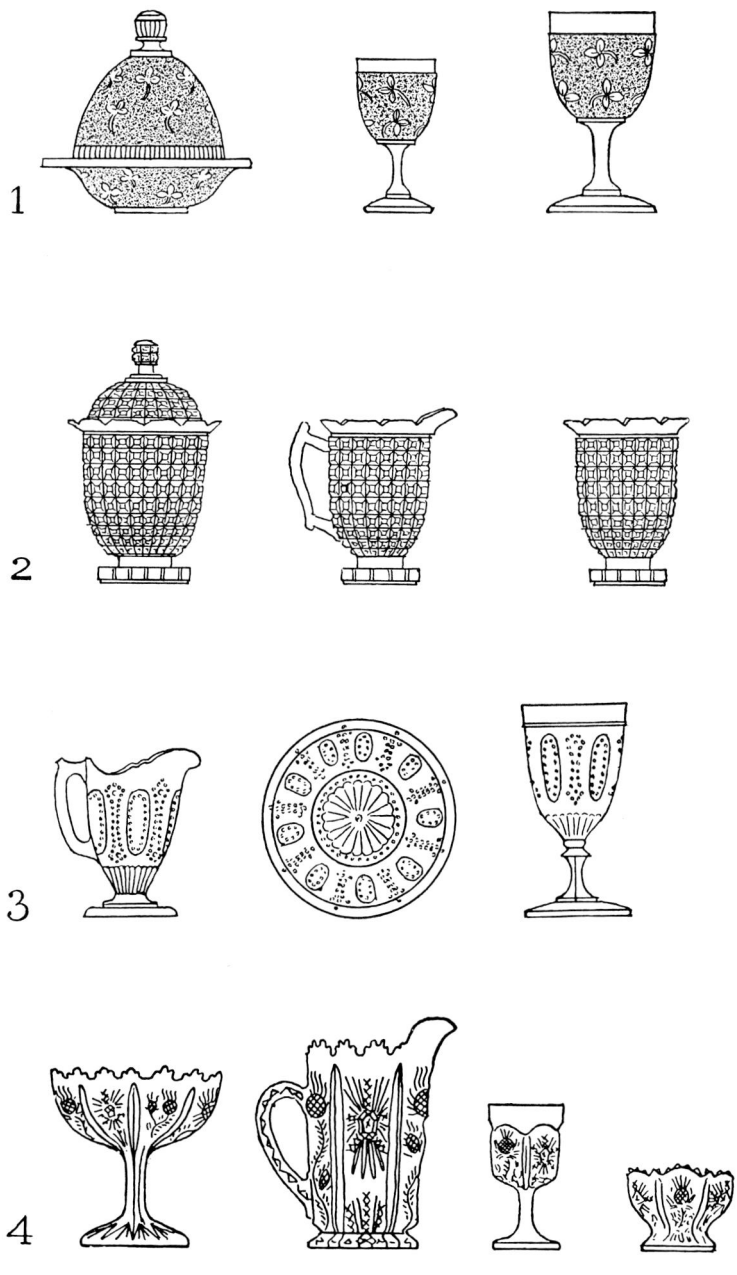

PLATE 141
1. STIPPLED CLOVER butter dish, cordial, goblet.
2. MILK-WHITE WAFFLE sugar bowl, creamer, spoonholder.
3. "101" creamer, plate, goblet.
4. PANELED THISTLE compote, water pitcher, cordial, salt.

PLATE 142—GOBLETS

Blackberry
Strawberry

Currant
Barberry

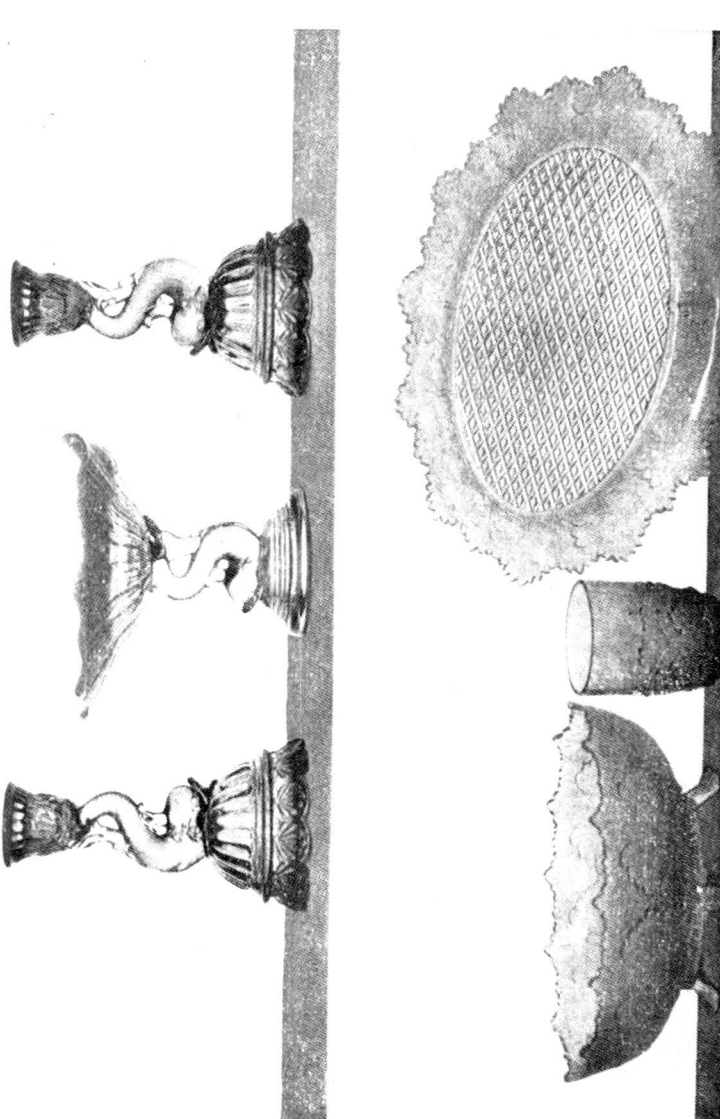

PLATE 143
Dolphin compote and Petticoat Dolphin candlesticks
Maple Leaf oval bowl, tumbler and platter

PLATE 144—LARGE PLATES

Diamond Cut with Leaf Odd Daisy bread plate
Grant Peace plate Maple Leaf plate

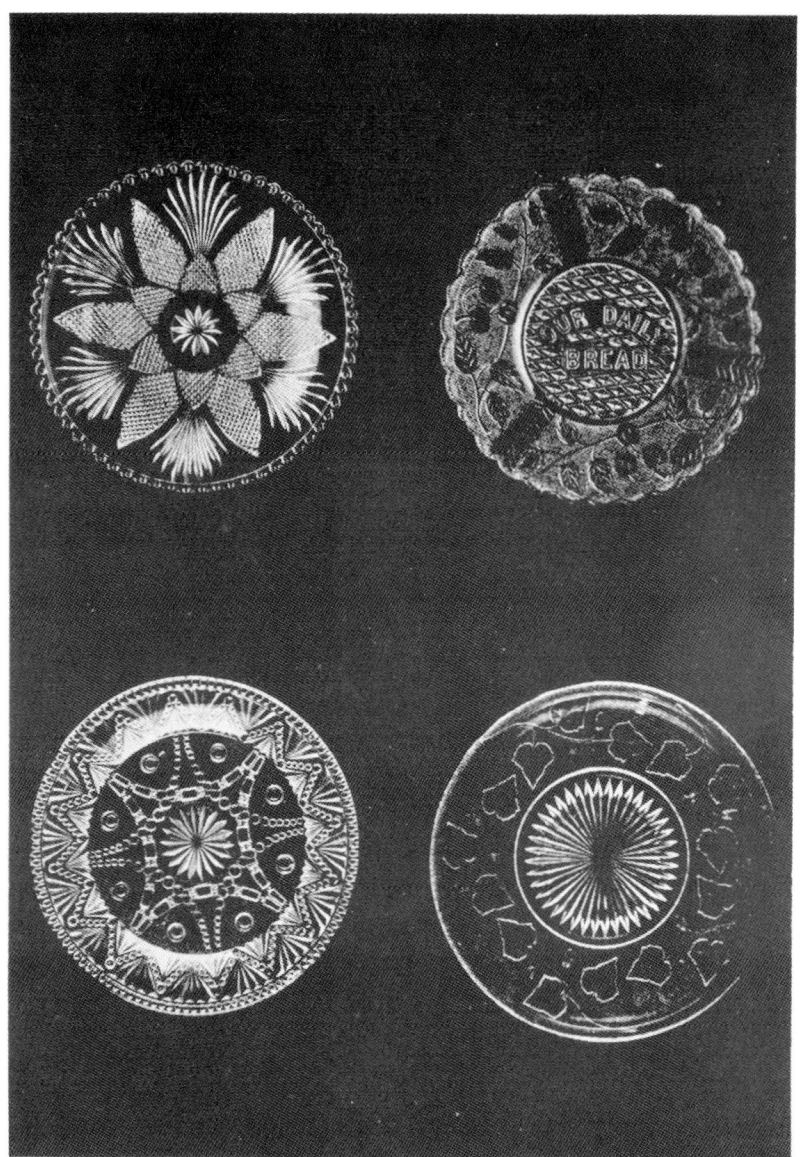

PLATE 145—LARGE PLATES

Teasel
Festoon

Stippled Cherry
Ivy in Snow

PLATE 146—GOBLETS

Thousand Eye Cathedral
Swirl Stippled Ivy

PLATE 147
1. RIBBED OPAL berry bowl, sauce dish, mug.
2. RIBBED OPAL creamer, pitcher, tall tumbler.
3. SPIRALLED IVY sugar bowl, spoonholder, water pitcher, tumbler.
4. STIPPLED STAR celery vase, sugar bowl, goblet.

PLATE 148—GOBLETS

Loop and Dart, diamond ornaments
Double Loop and Dart

Loop and Dart, round ornaments
Loop and Dart

PLATE 149

1. LEAF and DART celery vase, footed tumbler, creamer, footed salt.
2. LOOP and DART (round ornaments) creamer, celery vase, spoonholder, cordial.
3. LOOP and DART creamer, goblet, cordial, egg cup.
4. LOOP and DART (diamond ornaments) sugar bowl, butter dish, tumbler, water pitcher.

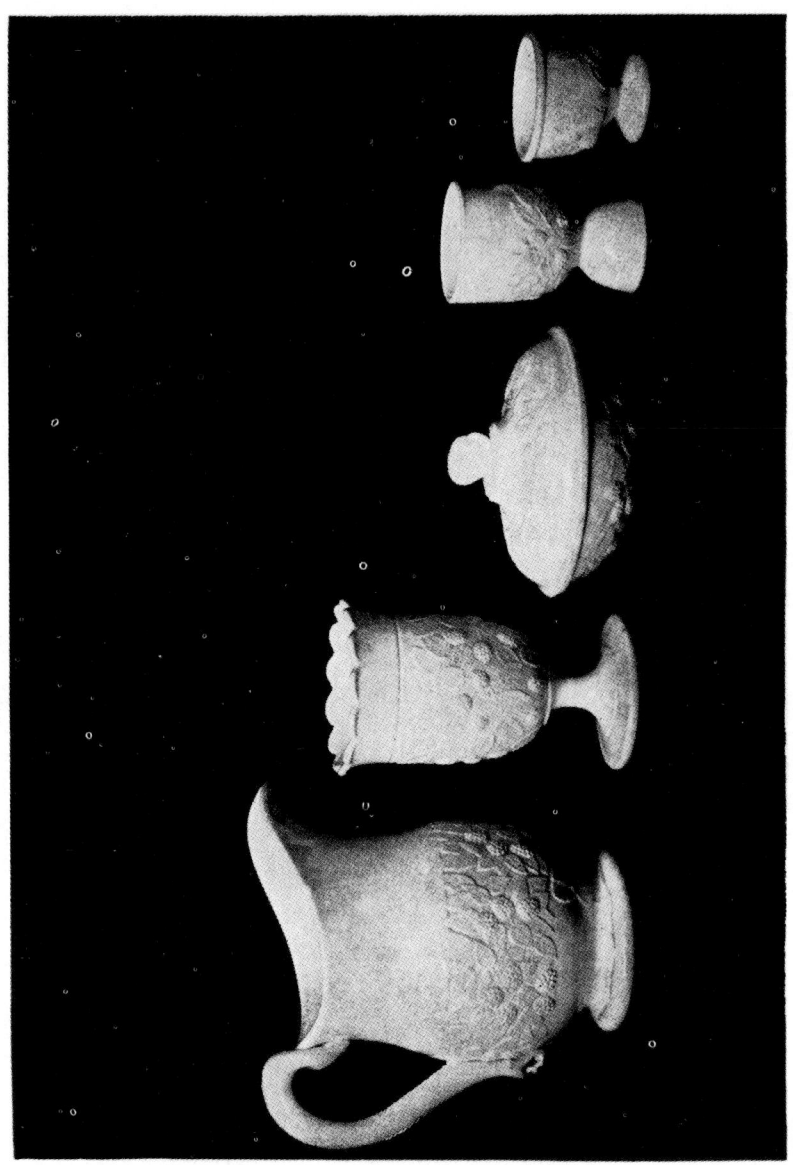

PLATE 150—MILK-WHITE BLACKBERRY

Water pitcher Celery vase Butter dish Egg cup Salt, footed

PLATE 151

1. STRAWBERRY and CURRANT goblet (showing both sides of bowl), butter dish
2. LOGANBERRY and GRAPE goblet (showing both sides of bowl), water pitcher.
3. STRAWBERRY creamer, sugar bowl, spoonholder, egg cup.
4. BLACKBERRY celery vase, spoonholder, footed salt.

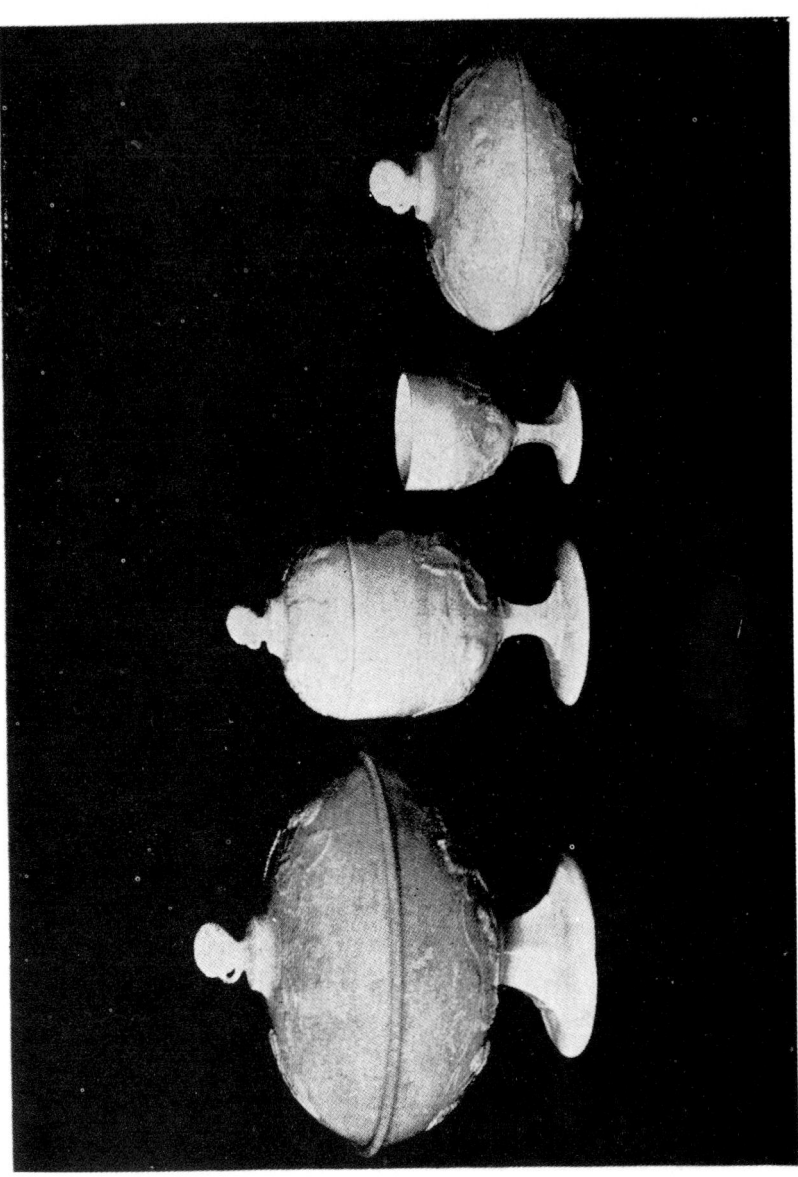

PLATE 152—MILK-WHITE STRAWBERRY

Covered compote   Sugar bowl   Egg cup   Butter dish

PLATE 153—GOBLETS
Including many odd patterns not collectible in other forms.

PLATE 154—GOBLETS
Including many odd patterns not collectible in other forms.

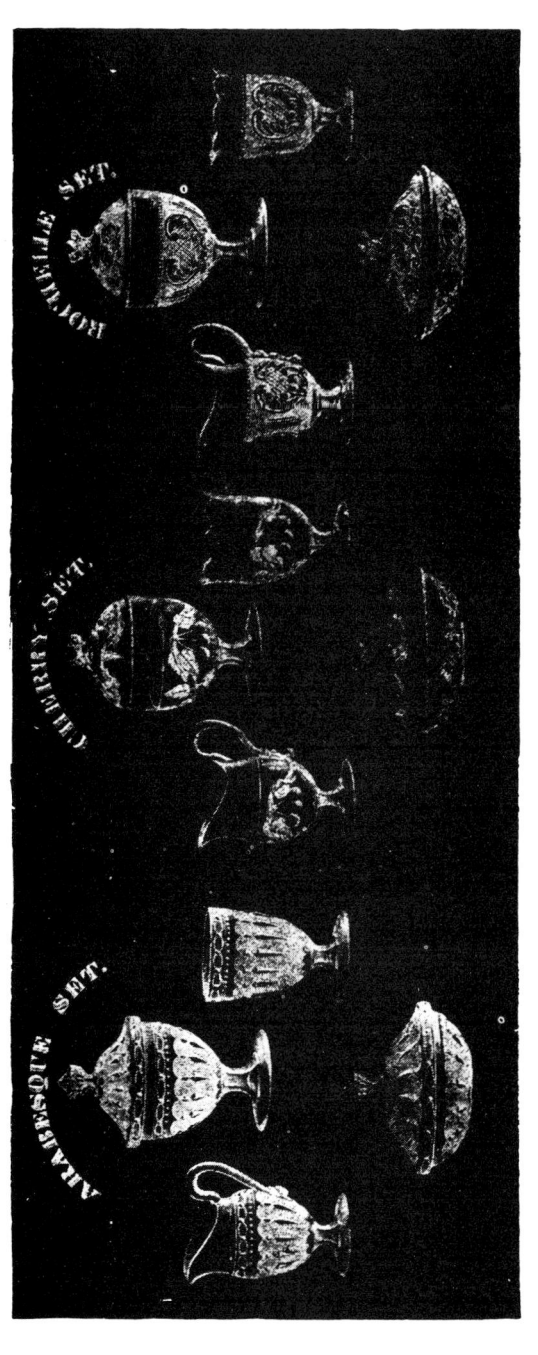

PLATE 155

Arabesque, Cherry and Rochelle (now termed Princess Feather) "sets," as taken from page of an old trade catalogue of Bakewell, Pears & Co.

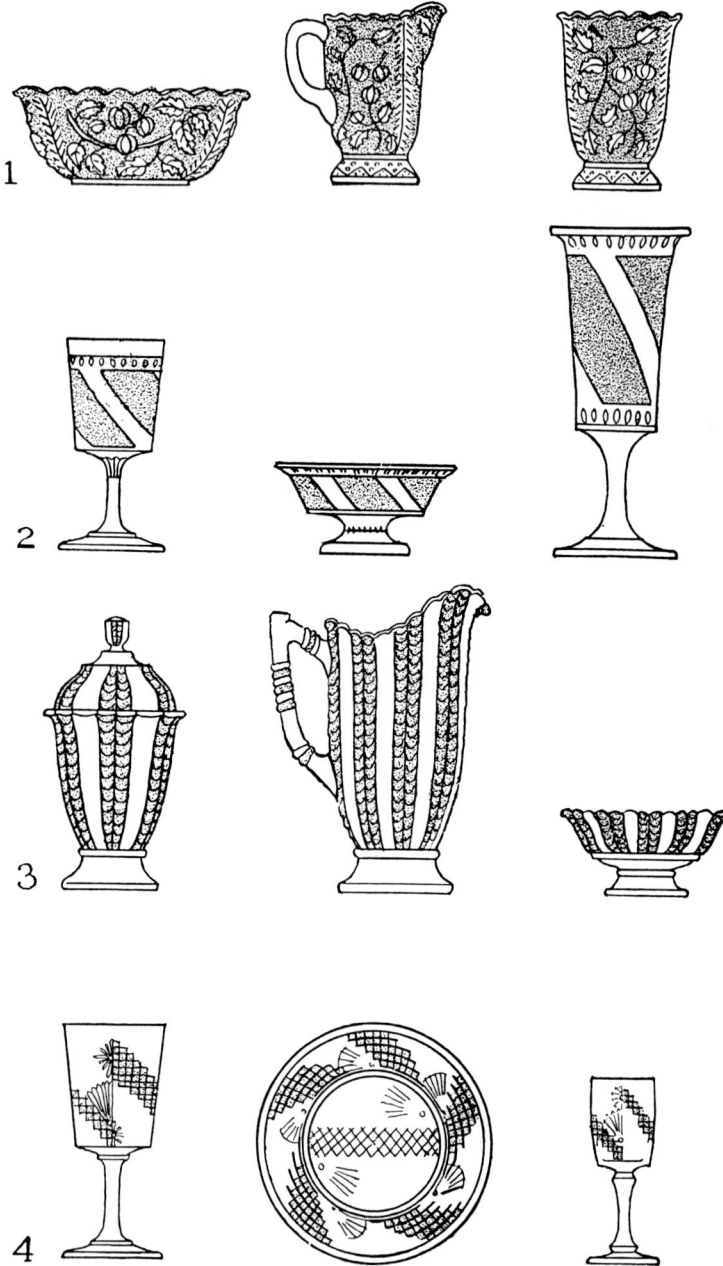

PLATE 156
1. STIPPLED CHERRY berry bowl, creamer, celery vase.
2. CLEAR DIAGONAL BAND goblet, footed sauce, celery vase.
3. FISH SCALE sugar bowl, water pitcher, footed sauce.
4. DIAGONAL BAND with FAN goblet, plate, cordial.

PLATE 157

1. SHELL and TASSEL (square) tray, cake plate on standard, covered compote, footed sauce dish.
2. SHELL and TASSEL (round) sugar bowl, butter dish, celery vase.
3. PLEAT and PANEL sugar bowl, creamer. spoonholder, footed sauce dish.
4. ROMAN ROSETTE sugar bowl, creamer, spoonholder, butter dish.

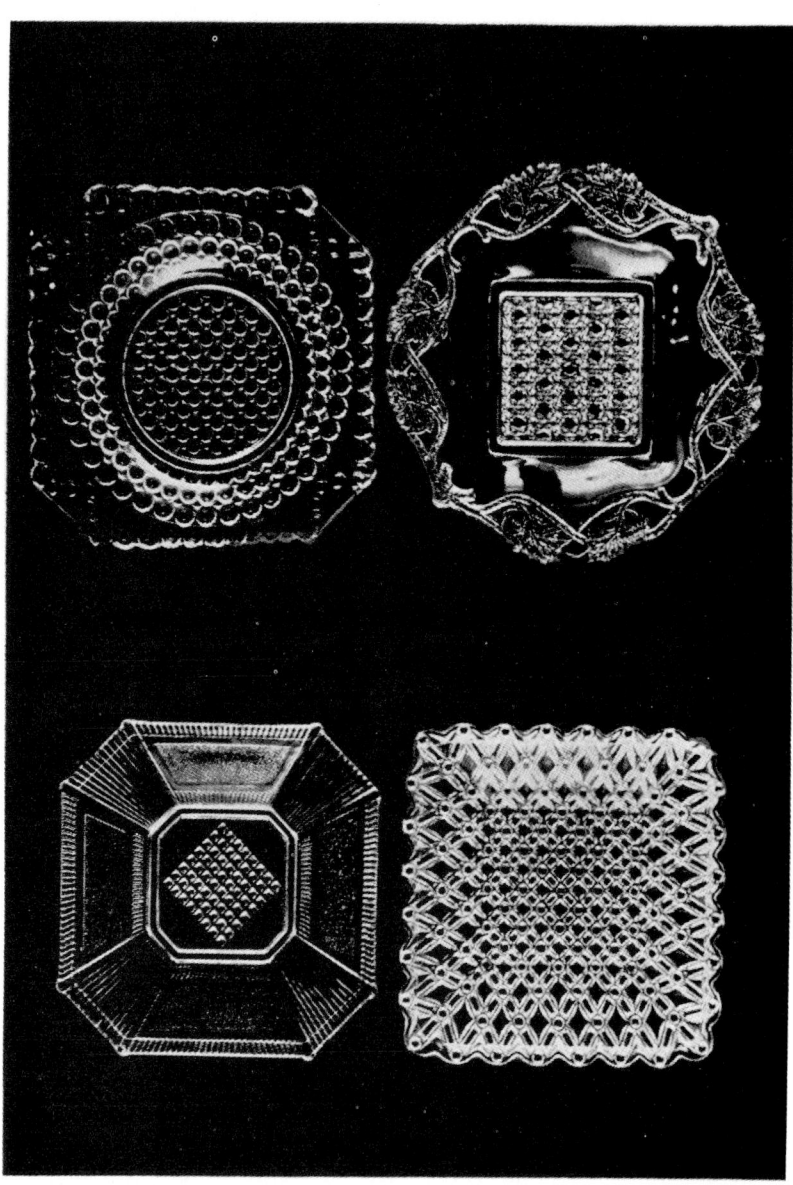

PLATE 158—SQUARE PLATES

Thousand-Eye Maple Leaf, variant
Pleat and Panel Nailhead

PLATE 159
1. MARQUISETTE goblet, compote on high foot, spoonholder.
2. WILLOW OAK water pitcher, creamer, goblet.
3. TWO-PANEL creamer, sugar bowl, celery vase.
4. THREE-PANEL celery vase, butter dish, creamer, footed sauce dish.

PLATE 160—GOBLETS

Two Panel Fine Cut

Fine Cut and Panel Cane

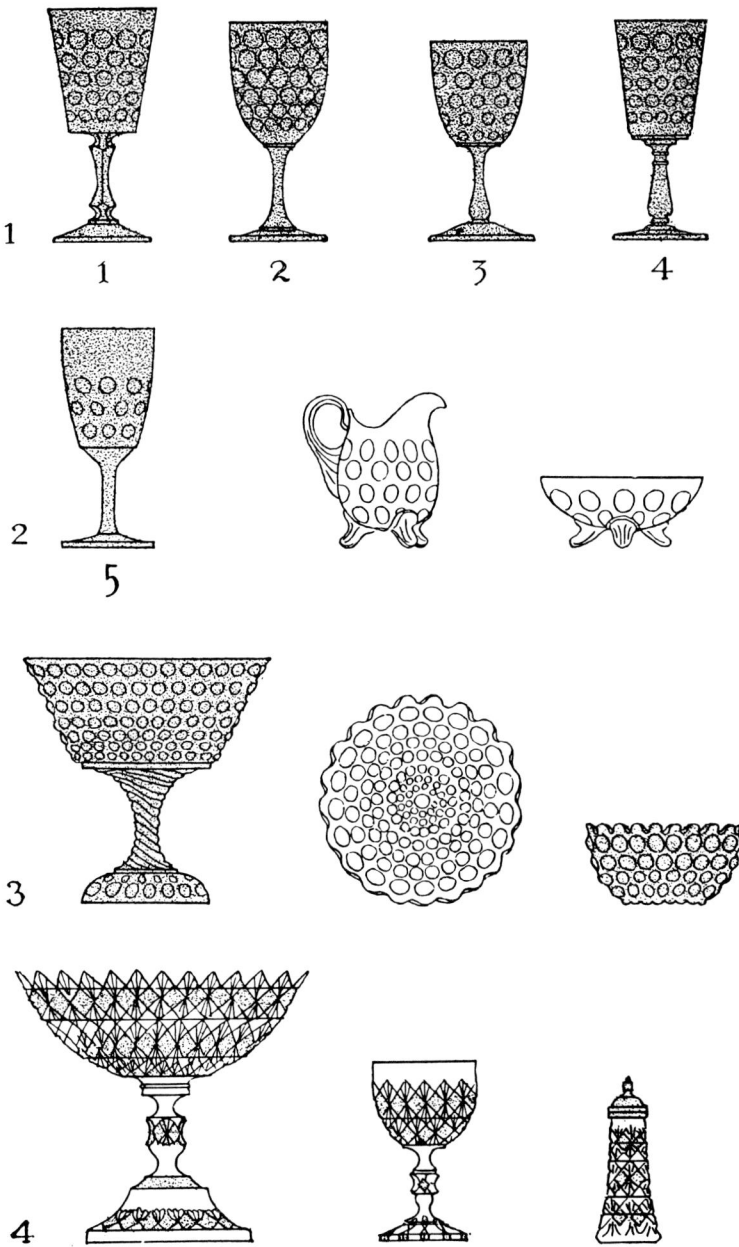

PLATE 161
1. INVERTED THUMBPRINT goblets. Variants.
2. INVERTED THUMBPRINT goblet, creamer, sauce dish.
3. RAINDROP compote, plate, finger bowl.
4. FINE CUT and BLOCK compote, goblet, salt shaker.

PLATE 162

1. CRANBERRY RED INVERTED THUMBPRINT celery vase, small celery holder, tumbler, wine, punch cup.
2. INVERTED THUMBPRINT. Three varieties of finger bowls; large, with base; medium and small.
3. RED BLOCK goblet, sugar bowl, cordial.
4. RUBY THUMBPRINT goblet, spoonholder, pint pitcher, celery vase.

PLATE 163—PLATES

Ray
Maple Leaf, variant

Swirl
Daisy and Button

PLATE 164—GOBLETS
Including some patterns not collectible in other forms.

PLATE 165—MEMORIAL AND CAMPAIGN PLATES

Garfield Memorial Garfield Drape
Grant Cleveland and Hendricks

PLATE 166
1. SOUTHERN IVY water pitcher, sauce dish, berry bowl.
2. BUCKLE with STAR goblet, sauce dish, pickle dish.
3. FESTOON spoonholder, sauce dish, creamer.
4. GOOSEBERRY goblet, tumbler, spoonholder.

PLATE 167—GOBLETS

Variant of Daisy and Button with V ornament
Daisy and Button
Daisy and Button with Crossbar
Daisy and Button with Thumbprint

PLATE 168—DAISY AND BUTTON TUMBLERS

With Thumbprint
Crossbar with Thumbprint

With V ornament
Crossbar with pointed ornaments

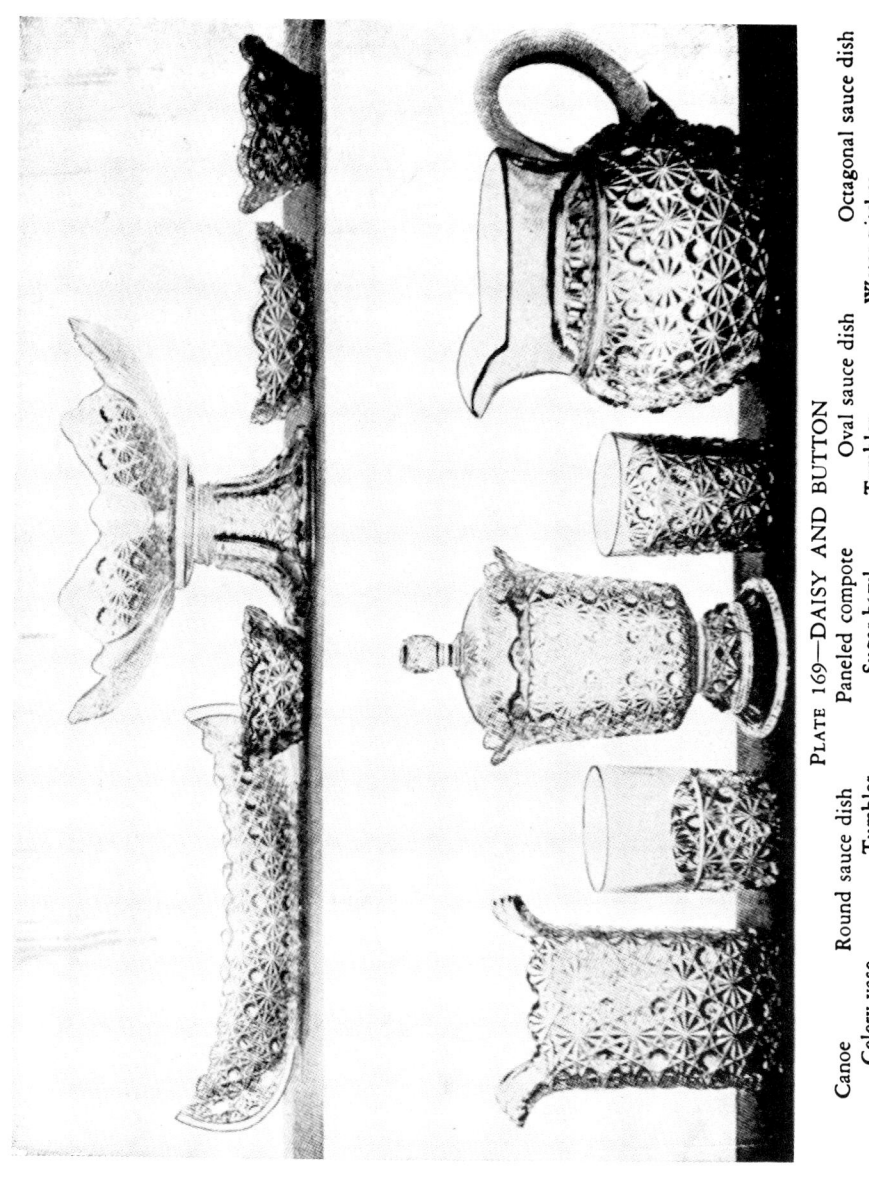

Canoe Round sauce dish Paneled compote Oval sauce dish Octagonal sauce dish
Celery vase Tumbler Sugar bowl Tumbler Water pitcher

PLATE 169—DAISY AND BUTTON

PLATE 170—DAISY AND BUTTON
Crossbar celery vase   Butter dish   Creamer   Water pitcher
With Thumbprint, compote on high standard   Compote on low standard   Cake plate on standard

PLATE 171—DAISY AND BUTTON
Compote on high standard   Castor set in plain pressed pattern
Finger bowl   Sherbet cup   Oblong deep dish
Paneled berry bowl
Celery vase, V ornaments

PLATE 172—MILK-WHITE PANELED WHEAT PATTERN COMPOTE AND BUTTER DISH

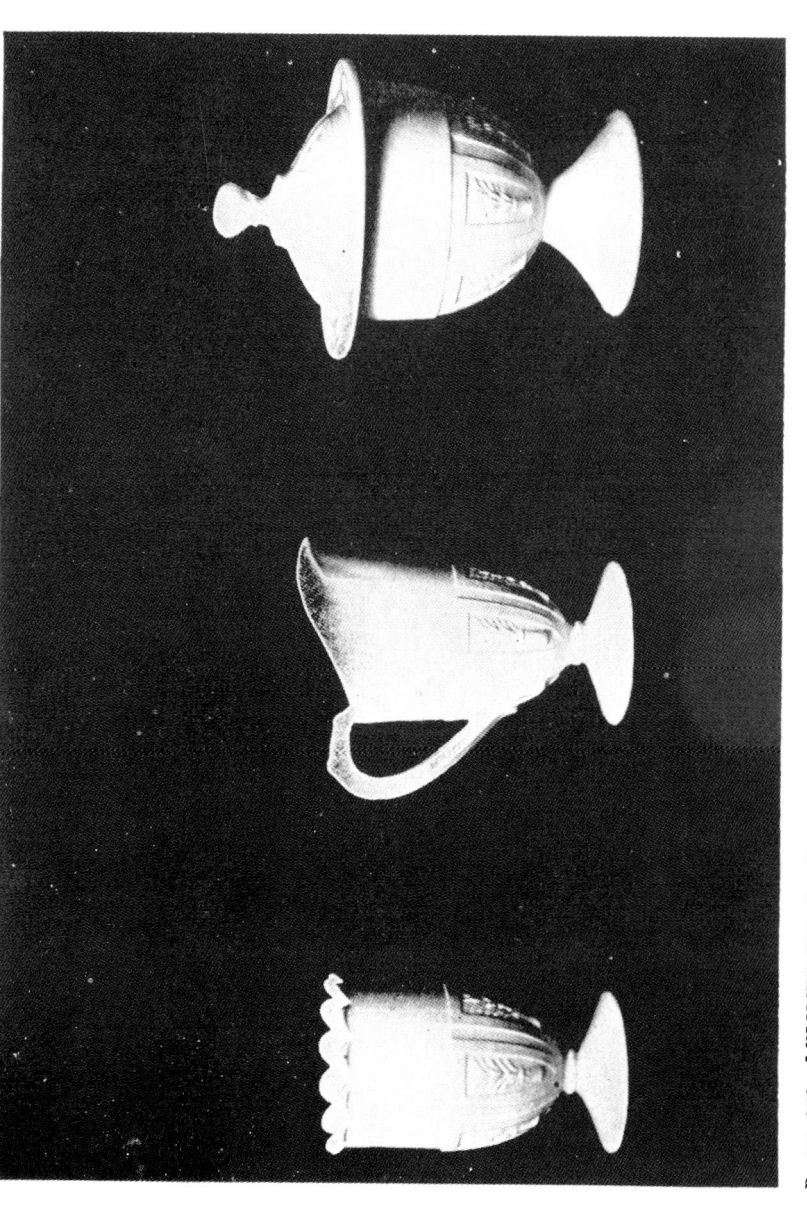

PLATE 173—MILK-WHITE PANELED WHEAT PATTERN SPOONHOLDER, CREAMER AND SUGAR BOWL

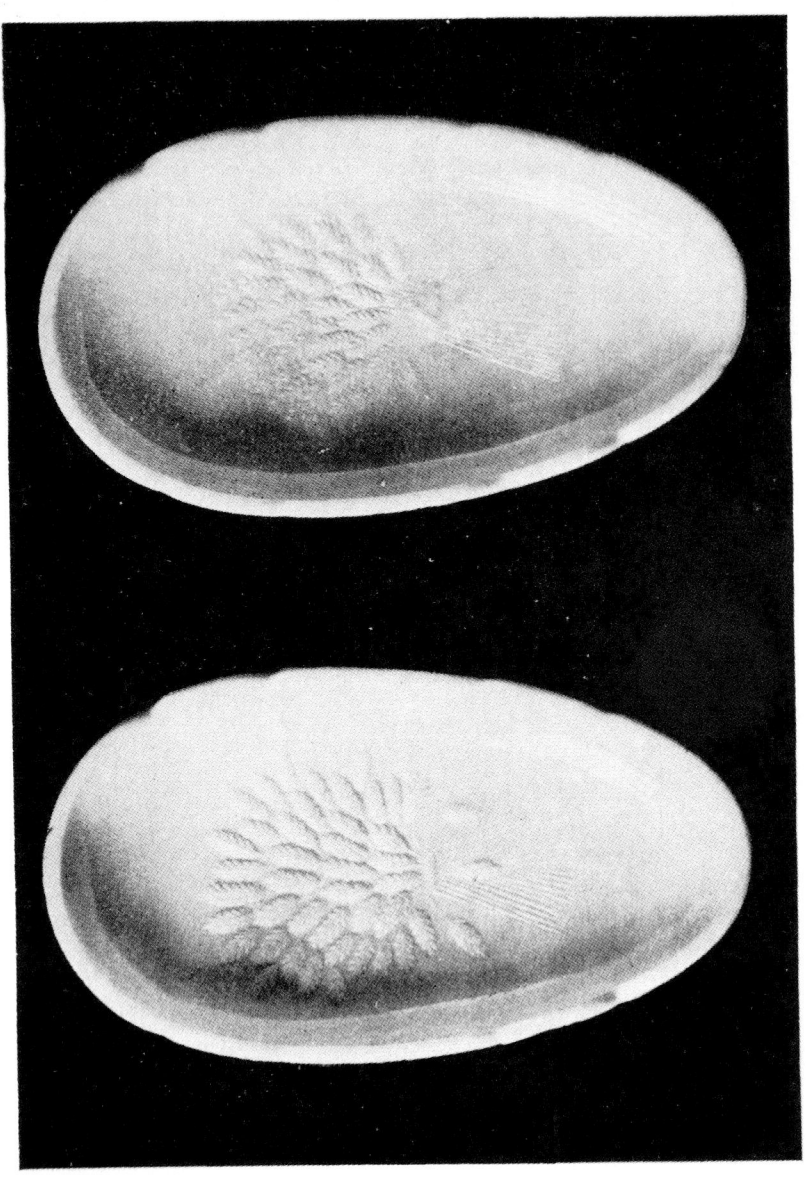

Collection of Dr. Charles Ferris.

PLATE 173A—MILK-WHITE WHEAT RELISH DISH, SHOWING THE TWO VARIATIONS

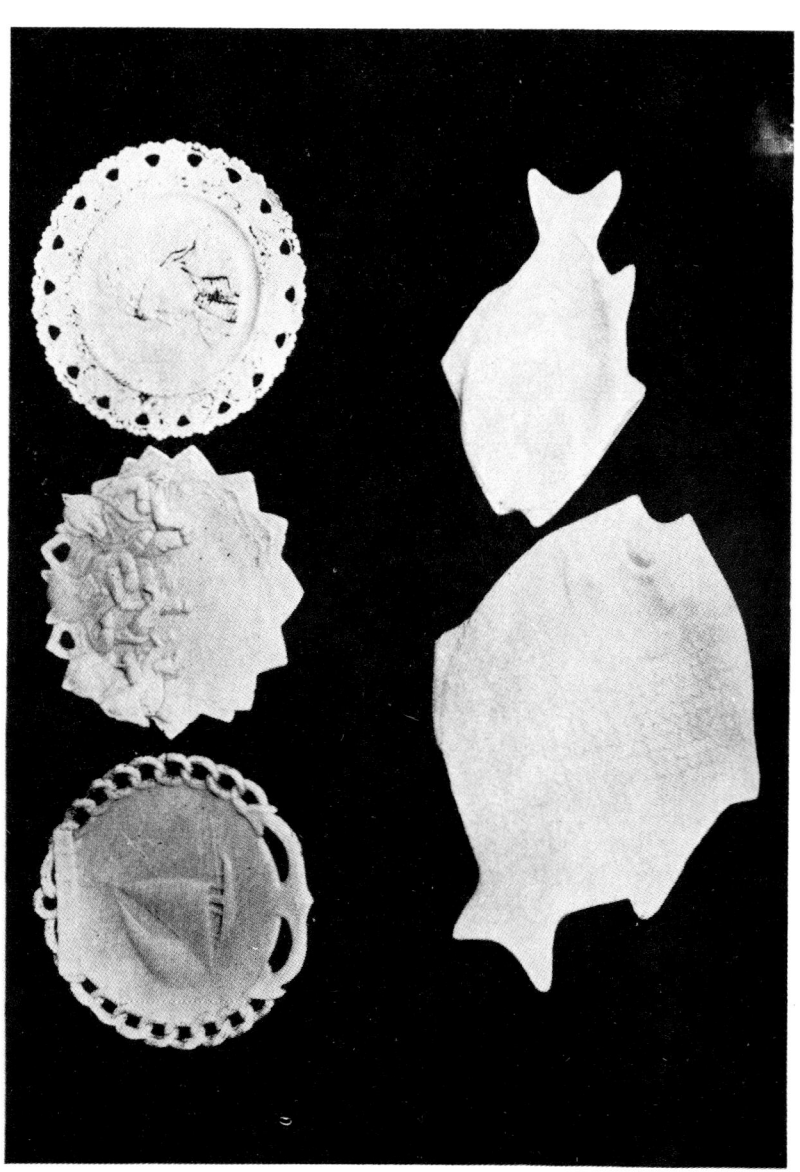

PLATE 174.—MILK-WHITE PLATES AND FISH PLATTERS

PLATE 175—MILK-WHITE "LACE EDGED" BOWLS

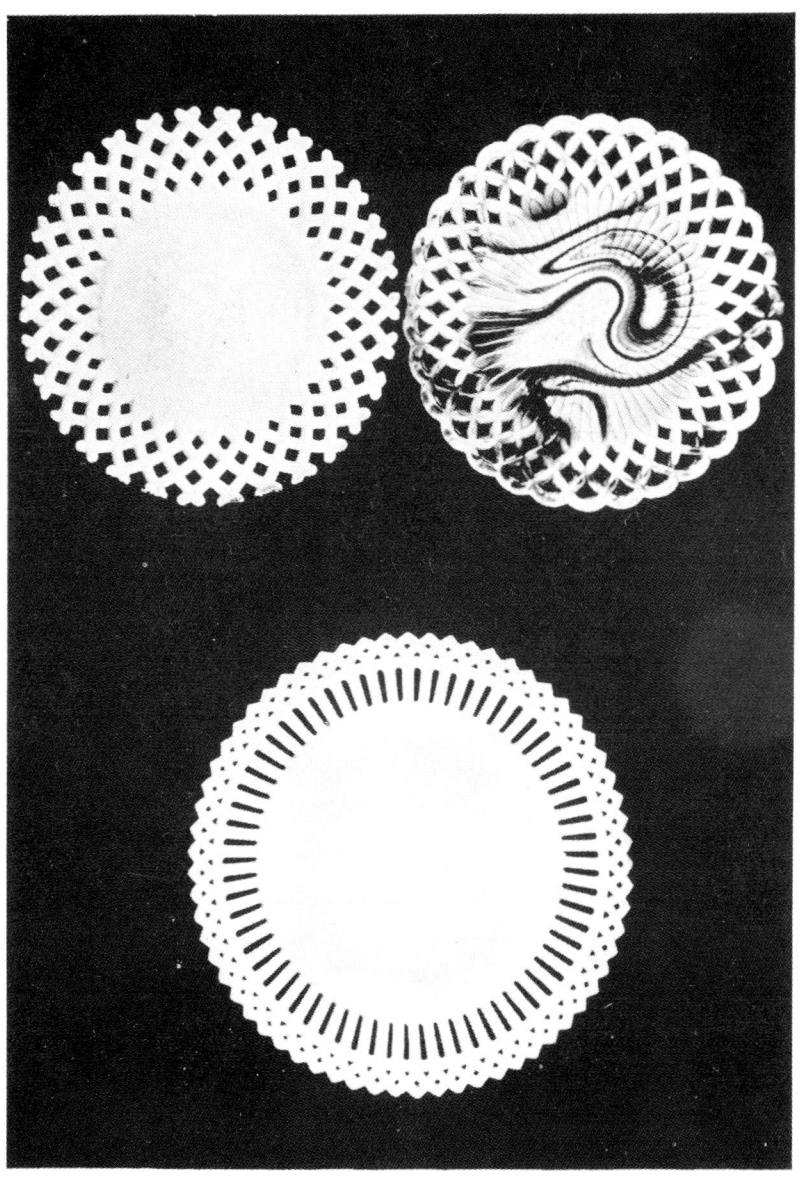

PLATE 176—LARGE PLATES
Lattice edge in milk-white   Open edge in Marble glass
Milk-white plate with Gothic border
(See page 619)

PLATE 177

MILK-WHITE VASES IN ROSE PATTERN   GOBLET AND PLATE IN OPAQUE CREAM COLOR

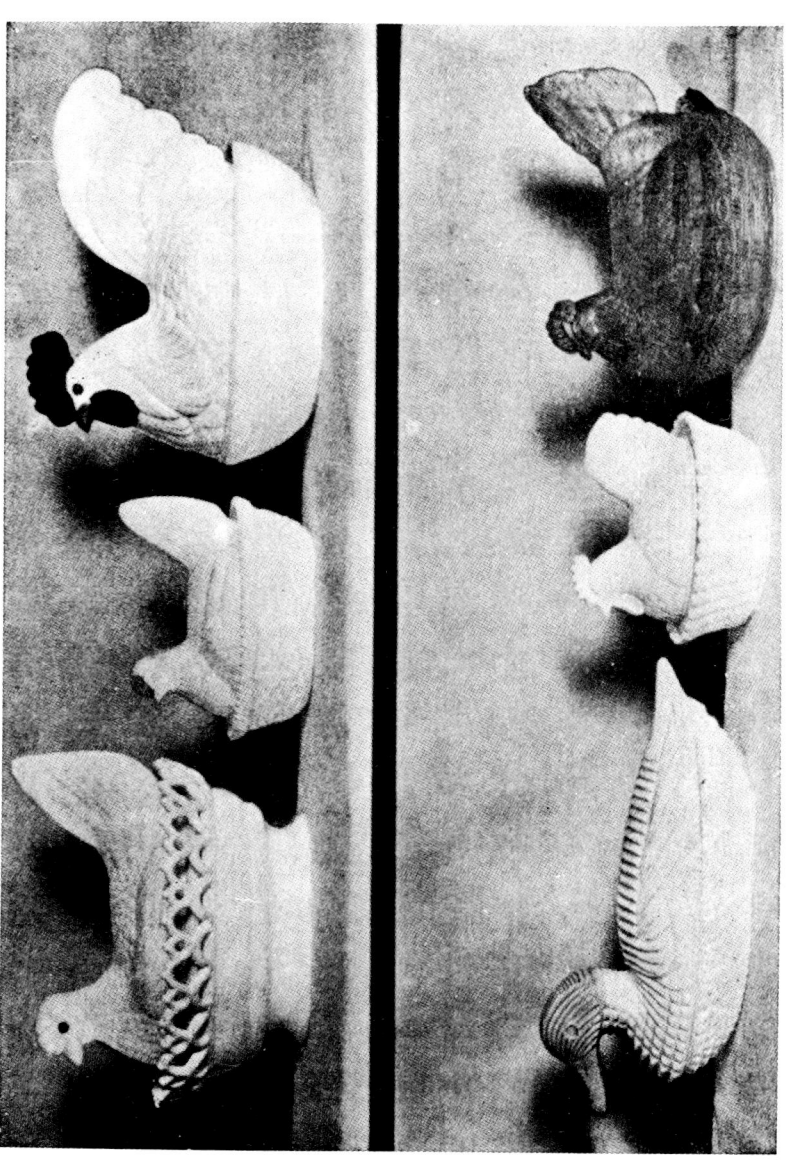

PLATE 178—MILK-WHITE COVERED DISHES
(See page 609)

PLATE 179—MARBLE GLASS IN FLUTED PATTERN

Butter dish Compote Oblong deep dish

PLATE 180—MARBLE GLASS
Tumbler Celery vase Vase Goblet
Match holder Creamer Spoonholder Boot match holder
(Creamer and spoonholder in yellow and white marbelized glass)

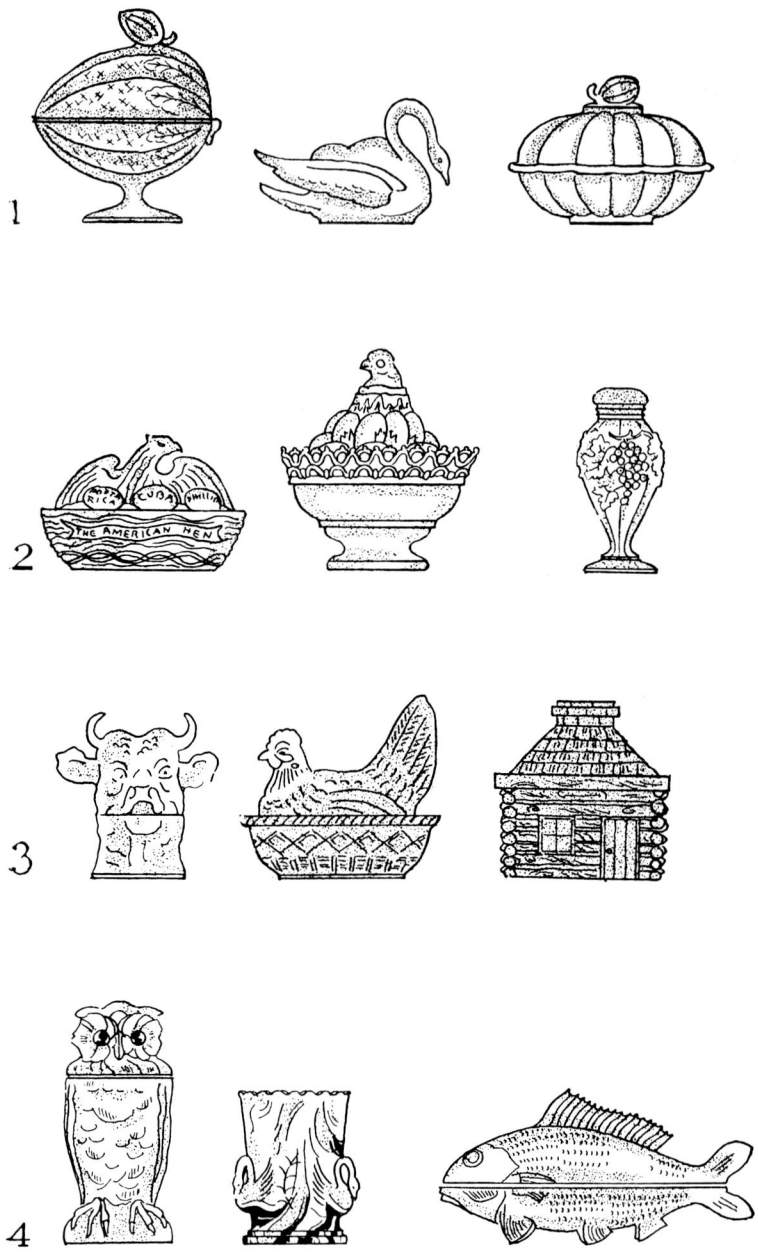

PLATE 181
1. MILK-WHITE covered melon dish, SWAN salt, covered melon dish.
2. MILK-WHITE eagle covered dish, hen lace-edged covered dish, GRAPE salt.
3. Cow mustard jar, hen covered dish, log cabin.
4. OPAQUE BLUE OWL, yellow and white MARBLE glass spoonholder, FISH covered dish.

(See page 609)

PLATE 182—MILK-WHITE PLATES
(See page 616)

 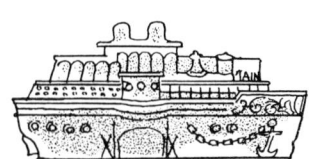 

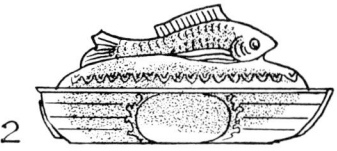 

PLATE 183

1. MILK-WHITE tall eagle inscribed "E Pluribus Unum"; battleship Maine, small covered hen dish.
2. MILK-WHITE dish with fish on cover, dish with turtle on cover.
3. MILK-WHITE sleigh with hen on cover, dish with lion on cover.
4. MILK-WHITE battleship with Uncle Sam on cover, dish with head of Admiral Dewey on cover.

(See page 609)

PLATE 184

Page from Bakewell, Pears & Co. catalogue illustrating their opaque "Rochelle" pattern. This is now known as Princess Feather.

PLATE 185—KNIGHTS OF LABOR PLATTER

PLATE 186

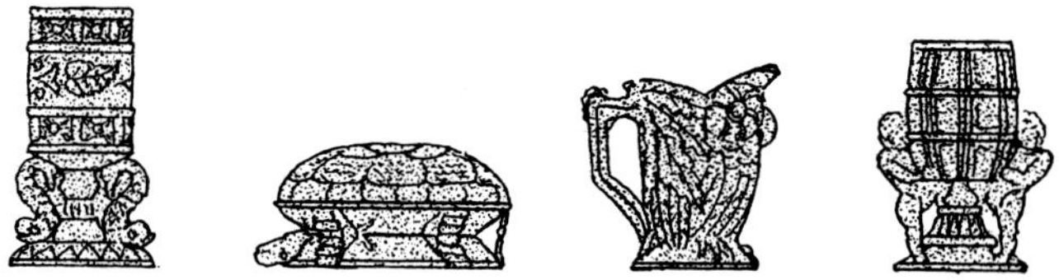

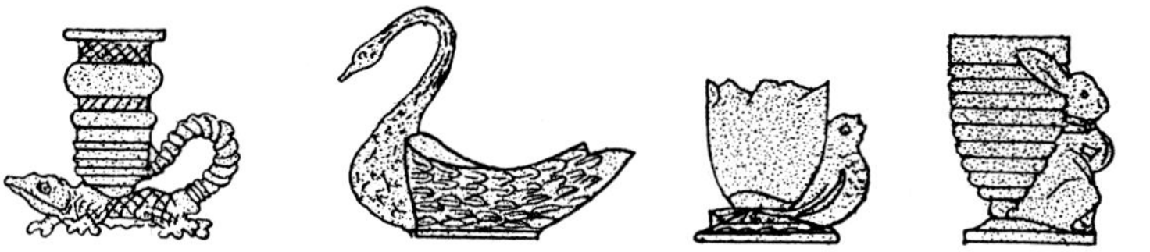

1. DOLPHIN match holder, TURTLE salt, OWL creamer, CHERUB match holder.
2. ALLIGATOR match holder, SWAN salt, CHICKEN toothpick holder, RABBIT match holder.
3. KITTEN match holder, BIRD mustard jar, MONKEY toothpick holder, ROOSTER salt.
4. ROOSTER match holder, DOG match holder, DOG salt, SWAN salt.

(See page 625)

PLATE 187—LARGE PLATES

Late Thistle
Open edge, with basket weave center

Block with fan border
Double vine

(See page 645)

PLATE 188
DEEP DISH WITH SHEAF OF WHEAT IN CENTER
LARGE TRAY WITH SCENE DEPICTING NIAGARA FALLS
(See page 645)

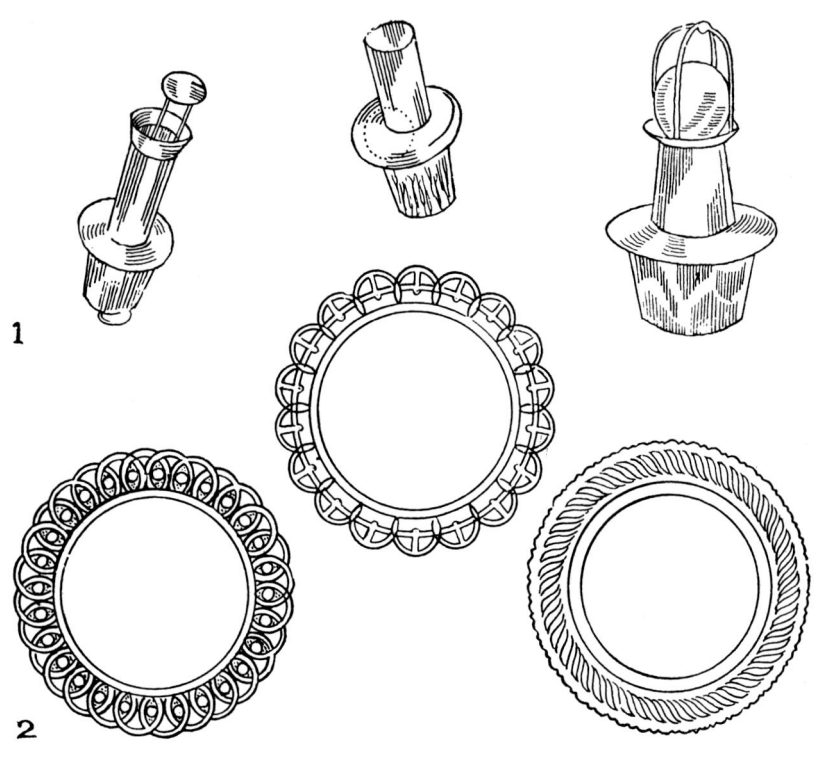

PLATE 189
PATENT CORKS
MILK-WHITE PLATES

PLATE 190—ODDS AND ENDS
1. BIRD creamer, crossed fern sauce dish, swan salt.
2. PICKLE jar, double vine relish dish, shell spoonholder.
3. Bakewell, Pears & Co.'s "THISTLE" decanter and water pitcher, draped star sauce dish, butterfly salt.
4. MILK-WHITE plate, stippled chain salt, rare purple marble glass candlestick.

INDEX

Acorn, group in line drawings *Plate* 125
Acorn variants, in line drawings *Plate* 125
Anthemion, group in line drawings *Plate* 58
Arabesque compote *Plate* 23
Arabesque, goblet *Plate* 121
Arabesque, group from old catalogue *Plate* 155
Arched Grape, group in line drawings *Plate* 64
Arched Leaf, goblet *Plate* 28
Arched Leaf, plate *Plate* 73
Argus goblet *Plate* 2
Argus, group in line drawings *Plate* 11
Ashburton goblet *Plate* 1
Ashburton, group in line drawings *Plate* 3
Baby Face, group in line drawings *Plate* 89
Baltimore Pear, group in line drawings *Plate* 66
Band, group in line drawings *Plate* 61
Banded Buckle, goblet *Plate* 62
Banded Buckle, group in line drawings *Plate* 102
Bar tumblers. Group from old catalogue *Plate* 8
Barberry goblet *Plate* 142
Barberry, group in line drawings *Plate* 139
Barberry six inch plate *Plate* 135
Barley, group in line drawings *Plate* 116
Barley six inch plate *Plate* 113
Barred Forget-me-not, group in line drawings *Plate* 132
Barred Forget-me-not, large plate *Plate* 131
Basket Weave, group in line drawings *Plate* 104
Beaded Acorn, group in line drawings *Plate* 65
Beaded Acorn six inch plate *Plate* 124
Beaded Band, group in line drawings *Plate* 61
Beaded Dewdrop goblet *Plate* 57
Beaded Grape, group in line drawings *Plate* 63
Beaded Grape Medallion, group in line drawings *Plate* 66
Beaded Grape Medallion (banded) group in line drawings *Plate* 66
Beaded Loop, group in line drawings *Plate* 76
Beaded Oval and Scroll, group in line drawings *Plate* 77
Beaded Tulip, group in line drawings *Plate* 116
Beaded Tulip plate *Plate* 44
Bear jar *Plate* 127
Bellflower details *Plate* 31
Bellflower, full page of line drawings *Plate* 30
Bellflower goblet *Plate* 33
Bellflower opal egg cups *Plate* 35
Bellflower plate *Plate* 32
Bellflower rarities in line drawings *Plate* 34
Bellflower sugar bowl *Plate* 31A
Bellflower variants in line drawings *Plate* 34
Bigler, group in line drawings *Plate* 10

Index

Bird salt — *Plate* 127
Blackberry goblet — *Plate* 142
Blackberry, group in line drawings — *Plate* 151
Blackberry (milk white) group — *Plate* 150
Blaze, group in line drawings — *Plate* 13
Bleeding Heart goblet — *Plate* 123
Bleeding Heart, group in line drawings — *Plate* 128
Block with fan border, large plate — *Plate* 187
Block with Thumbprint, group showing a later variation in line drawings — *Plate* 101
Buckle goblet — *Plate* 62
Buckle, group in line drawings — *Plate* 102
Buckle with Star, group in line drawings — *Plate* 166
Budded Ivy, group in line drawings — *Plate* 119
Bull's Eye goblet — *Plate* 48
Bull's Eye, group in line drawings — *Plate* 49
Bull's Eye with Diamond Point goblet — *Plate* 27
Bull's Eye with Diamond Point group in line drawings — *Plate* 49
Bull's Eye with Fleur de Lys goblet — *Plate* 48
Bull's Eye with Fleur de Lys group — *Plate* 51
Bull's Eye variant in line drawings — *Plate* 50

Cabbage Leaf, group in line drawings — *Plate* 65
Cabbage Rose, group in line drawings — *Plate* 122
Cable, group in line drawings — *Plate* 36
Cable plate — *Plate* 32
Cable with Ring, group in line drawings — *Plate* 58
Canadian goblet — *Plate* 111
Canadian, group in line drawings — *Plate* 112
Canadian six inch plate — *Plate* 113
Cane goblet — *Plate* 160
Cane, group in line drawings — *Plate* 132
Cape Cod large plate — *Plate* 114
Cape Cod, group in line drawings — *Plate* 115
Cardinal Bird goblet — *Plate* 98
Cardinal Bird, group in line drawings — *Plate* 100
Cathedral goblet — *Plate* 146
Cathedral, group in line drawings — *Plate* 58
Centennial platter — *Plate* 118
Chain, group in line drawings — *Plate* 132
Chain and Shield platter — *Plate* 105
Chain and Shield, groups in line drawings — *Plate* 106
Chain with Star, group in line drawings — *Plate* 132
Cherry, group from old catalogue — *Plate* 19
Cherry, group from old catalogue — *Plate* 155
Cherry, group in line drawings — *Plate* 66
Classic goblet — *Plate* 98
Classic, group — *Plate* 97
Clear Diagonal Band, group in line drawings — *Plate* 156
Clear Ribbon, group in line drawings — *Plate* 70
Clematis, group in line drawings — *Plate* 75
Cleveland and Hendricks, oblong tray — *Plate* 165
Colonial goblet — *Plate* 2
Colonial, group in line drawings — *Plate* 10
Comet goblet — *Plate* 48
Comet, group in line drawings — *Plate* 49
Compotes, from an old catalogue — *Plate* 17

Index

Compotes having frosted birds as knobs to covers	Plate 99
Continental, from an old catalogue	Plate 15
Cord and Tassel, group in line drawings	Plate 116
Cranberry red Inverted Thumbprint, group in line drawings	Plate 162
Crystal goblet	Plate 2
Crystal, group from an old catalogue	Plate 9
Crystal, group from an old catalogue	Plate 9A
Cube goblet	Plate 26
Cupid and Venus bread tray	Plate 92
Cupid and Venus goblet	Plate 111
Cupid and Venus, group in line drawings	Plate 70
Currant goblet	Plate 142
Currant, group in line drawings	Plate 139
Currier and Ives tray	Plate 110
Curtain group	Plate 85
Dahlia goblet	Plate 130
Dahlia, group in line drawings	Plate 126
Dahlia, large plate	Plate 129
Dahlia platter	Plate 105
Dahlia, seven inch plate	Plate 138
Daisy and Button goblet	Plate 167
Daisy and Button, large group	Plate 169
Daisy and Button plate	Plate 87
Daisy and Button plate	Plate 134
Daisy and Button plate	Plate 163
Daisy and Button with Crossbar goblet	Plate 167
Daisy and Button with Crossbar, group	Plate 170
Daisy and Button, Panelled, group	Plate 171
Daisy and Button with Thumbprint, goblet	Plate 167
Daisy and Button with Thumbprint, group	Plate 170
Daisy and Button Variant goblet	Plate 167
Daisy and Button with V ornament, group	Plate 171
Daisy and Button tumbler, with Crossbar	Plate 168
Daisy and Button tumbler, Crossbar and Thumbprint	Plate 168
Daisy and Button with Thumbprint, tumbler	Plate 168
Daisy and Button tumbler, with V ornament	Plate 168
Daisy (odd) bread plate	Plate 144
Daisy plate	Plate 44
Deer and Dog group in line drawings	Plate 101
Deer and Pine Tree group	Plate 119
Dew with Raindrop goblet	Plate 57
Dew with Raindrop group in line drawings	Plate 69
Dewdrop goblet	Plate 71
Dewdrop in Points plate	Plate 87
Dewdrop with Sheaf of Wheat plate	Plate 73
Dewdrop with Star plate	Plate 73
Diagonal Band, group in line drawings	Plate 140
Diagonal Band with Fan group in line drawings	Plate 156
Diamond Band goblet	Plate 103
Diamond cut with Leaf goblet	Plate 109
Diamond cut with Leaf group in line drawings	Plate 108
Diamond cut with Leaf large plate	Plate 144
Diamond cut with Leaf seven inch plate	Plate 138
Diamond Point goblet	Plate 42
Diamond Point large group	Plate 43
Diamond Point plate	Plate 44
Diamond Point plate, star center	Plate 45
Diamond Point plate, star and circle center	Plate 45
Diamond Quilted, group in line drawings	Plate 104
Diamond Quilted with Bull's Eye border plate	Plate 52

Index

Diamond Sunburst group in line drawings *Plate* 78
Diamond Thumbprint group *Plate* 25
Diamond Thumbprint group in line drawings *Plate* 3
Dolphin candlesticks and compote *Plate* 143
Dolphin dish, Pittsburgh *Plate* 22
Dolphin dish in Ribbon pattern *Plate* 68
Double Loop and Dart goblet *Plate* 148
Double Loop group in line drawings *Plate* 101
Double Ribbon group in line drawings *Plate* 67
Double Spear group in line drawings *Plate* 132
Double Vine large plate *Plate* 187
Drapery goblet *Plate* 121
Drapery group in line drawings *Plate* 108

Egyptian goblet *Plate* 111
Egyptian platter *Plate* 118
English Hobnail group *Plate* 85
English Hobnail, panelled goblet
English Hobnail plate *Plate* 134
Plate 86
English Hobnail and Thumbprint group in line drawings *Plate* 14
English Hobnail and Thumbprint plate *Plate* 87
Etruscan from an old catalogue *Plate* 20
Eugenie group from an old catalogue *Plate* 5
Eureka group from an old catalogue *Plate* 6
Excelsior candlesticks *Plate* 34
Excelsior goblet *Plate* 1
Excelsior group in line drawings *Plate* 4
Excelsior group from an old catalogue *Plate* 7

Fan with Diamond group in line drawings *Plate* 76
Festoon group in line drawings *Plate* 166
Festoon large plate *Plate* 145
Fine Cut and Block group in line drawings *Plate* 161
Fine Cut and panel goblet *Plate* 160
Fine Cut and panel group in line drawings *Plate* 61
Fine Cut goblet *Plate* 160
Fine Cut seven inch plate *Plate* 138
Fine Rib goblet *Plate* 27
Fine Rib group in line drawings *Plate* 36
Fishscale goblet *Plate* 120
Fishscale group in line drawings *Plate* 156
Flattened Hobnail goblet *Plate* 71
Flattened Sawtooth group in line drawings *Plate* 65
Flower Band goblet *Plate* 109
Flower Band group in line drawings *Plate* 107
Flower Pot group in line drawings *Plate* 136
Flower Pot platter *Plate* 133
Flute goblet *Plate* 1
Flute group in line drawings *Plate* 13
Fluted Ribbon group in line drawings *Plate* 67
Forget-me-not in Scroll goblet *Plate* 86
Forget-me-not in Scroll group in line drawings *Plate* 77
Four Petal group in line drawings *Plate* 12
Frosted Circle goblet *Plate* 96
Frosted Circle group in line drawings *Plate* 76
Frosted Circle large plate *Plate* 131
Frosted Leaf group in line drawings *Plate* 94
Frosted Ribbon group in line drawings *Plate* 69

Index

Frosted Stork and other plates *Plate* 68
Frosted Stork group in line drawings *Plate* 100
Garfield Drape, goblet *Plate* 98
Garfield Drape group in line drawings *Plate* 104
Garfield Drape large plate *Plate* 165
Garfield Memorial large plate *Plate* 165
Garfield Plate (odd) *Plate* 52
Goblets, group from an old catalogue *Plate* 24
Goblets, group showing twenty in line drawings *Plate* 153
Goblets, group showing twenty in line drawings *Plate* 154
Goblets, group showing twenty in line drawings *Plate* 164
Gooseberry goblet *Plate* 103
Gooseberry group in line drawings *Plate* 166
Gothic group *Plate* 55
Grant Peace plate *Plate* 144
Grant Square plate (odd) *Plate* 165
Grape and Festoon (Stippled leaf) group in line drawings *Plate* 63
Grape Band, group in line drawings *Plate* 64
Grape bread plate *Plate* 118
Grape pattern, opaque cream color *Plate* 177
Grape six inch plate *Plate* 113

Hamilton, large group *Plate* 56
Hamilton with Leaf goblet *Plate* 57
Hand group in line drawings *Plate* 107
Harp group in line drawings *Plate* 14
Heavy Jewel group in line drawings *Plate* 137
Herringbone goblet *Plate* 121
Herringbone group in line drawings *Plate* 115

Historical platters *Plate* 117
Hobnail, large groups *Plates* 80, 81, 82, 83
Hobnail plates *Plate* 74, 88
Hobnail, English *Plate* 85
Hobnail, Opal, group in line drawings *Plate* 84
Hobnail, panelled, group in line drawings *Plate* 84
Hobnail with Fantop goblet *Plate* 71
Holly group in line drawings *Plate* 116
Honeycomb, full page of line drawings *Plate* 60
Honeycomb with Star group in line drawings *Plate* 102
Horn of Plenty goblet *Plate* 48
Horn of Plenty large group *Plate* 47
Horn of Plenty plate *Plate* 32
Horseshoe goblet *Plate* 130
Horseshoe group in line drawings *Plate* 112
Horseshoe large plate *Plate* 131
Horseshoe platter *Plate* 133
Huber group in line drawings *Plate* 11

Icicle, from old catalogues *Plate* 19, 20, 22
Inverted Fern goblet *Plate* 33
Inverted Fern group in line drawings *Plate* 36
Inverted Thumbprint finger bowls in line drawings *Plate* 162
Inverted Thumbprint goblets, variants in line drawings *Plate* 161
Inverted Thumbprint group in line drawings *Plate* 161
Ivy in Snow goblet *Plate* 103
Ivy in Snow group in line drawings *Plate* 119
Ivy in Snow large plate *Plate* 145

Jacob's Coat group in line drawings *Plate* 115
Jacob's Ladder goblet *Plate* 57

Index

Jacob's Ladder group in line drawings Plate 50
Jewel with Dewdrop group in line drawings Plate 75
Jumbo group in line drawings Plate 94
Knights of Labor platter Plate 185

Late Buckle goblet Plate 72
Late Panelled Grape group in line drawings Plate 65
Lattice group in line drawings Plate 78
Leaf and Dart celery vase Plate 95
Leaf and Dart group in line drawings Plate 149
Liberty Bell group in line drawings Plate 58
Liberty Bell six inch plate Plate 113
Lily of the Valley goblet Plate 123
Lily of the Valley group in line drawings Plate 126
Lincoln Drape goblet Plate 26
Lincoln Drape group in line drawings Plate 46
Lincoln Drape with Tassel goblet Plate 26
Lincoln Drape with Tassel group in line drawings Plate 46
Lion bread plate Plate 92
Lion, full page of line drawings Plate 93
Lion goblet Plate 91
Lion lamp Plate 90
Lion platter Plate 92
Log Cabin group in line drawings Plate 106
Loganberry and Grape group in line drawings Plate 151
Loop goblet Plate 1
Loop group in line drawings Plate 4
Loop and Dart goblet Plate 148
Loop and Dart (diamond ornaments) goblet Plate 148
Loop and Dart (diamond ornaments) group in line drawings Plate 149

Loop and Dart (diamond ornaments) plate Plate 124
Loop and Dart (double) goblet Plate 148
Loop and Dart (round ornaments) goblet Plate 148
Loop and Dart (round ornaments) group in line drawings Plate 149
Loop with Dewdrops group in line drawings Plate 79
Lord's Supper bread plate Plate 133

Magnet and Grape (frosted leaf) group in line drawings Plate 63
Magnet and Grape goblet Plate 62
Magnet and Grape wine jug Frontispiece
Maple Leaf group Plate 143
Maple Leaf large plate Plate 144
Maple Leaf, variant, plates Plate, 158, 163
Marble glass, Fluted Plate 179
Marble glass group Plate 180
Marble glass plate Plate 176
Marquisette group in line drawings Plate 159
Match holders Plate 127
Medallion group in line drawings Plate 102
Milk-White covered animal dishes Plate 178
Milk-White covered dishes in line drawings Plate 181, 183
Milk-White lace edged bowls Plate 175
Milk-White plates Plate 176, 182, 189
Milk-White plates and fish platters Plate 174
Milk-White vases, Rose pattern Plate 177
Milk-White Waffle group in line drawings Plate 141
Minerva goblet Plate 121
Minerva group in line drawings Plate 115
Mirror goblet Plate 2
Monkey group Plate 94A

Index

Moon and Star goblet Plate 103
Moon and Star group in line drawings Plate 69

Nailhead group in line drawings Plate 108
Nailhead plate Plate 158
New England Pineapple goblet Plate 42
New England Pineapple group in line drawings Plate 53
New England Pineapple plate Plate 52
Niagara Falls tray Plate 188

Odd seven inch plate Plate 134
Odds and ends in line drawings Plate 190
"101" goblet Plate 72
"101" group in line drawings Plate 141
"101" plate Plate 74
Open edge, basket weave center plate Plate 187
Open Rose goblet Plate 123
Open Rose group in line drawings Plate 122
Oval Mitre group in line drawings Plate 12
Oval Panel goblet Plate 62
Overshot Glass plate Plate 135
Owl and Possum group in line drawings Plate 100

Palmette celery vase Plate 95
Palmette goblet Plate 120
Palmette group in line drawings Plate 112
Palmette large plate Plate 129
Panelled cherry group in line drawings Plate 79
Panelled Daisy celery vase Plate 95
Panelled Daisy group in line drawings Plate 136
Panelled Daisy round plate Plate 135
Panelled Daisy square plate Plate 134
Panelled Dewdrop goblet Plate 72

Panelled Dewdrop group in line drawings Plate 75
Panelled Diamond Point goblet Plate 86
Panelled Diamond Point group in line drawings Plate 104
Panelled Flower, Stippled, group in line drawings Plate 77
Panelled Forget-me-not goblet Plate 130
Panelled Forget-me-not group in line drawings Plate 79
Panelled Forget-me-not platter Plate 133
Panelled Grape, group in line drawings Plate 64
Panelled Hobnail group Plate 84
Panelled Thistle group in line drawings Plate 141
Panelled Thistle plate Plate 114
Patent corks Plate 189
Peacock Feather (late) group in line drawings Plate 106
Petal and Loop group in line drawings Plate 4
Philadelphia group in line drawings Plate 61
Picket group in line drawings Plate 107
Pillar goblet Plate 28
Pinwheel plate Plate 44
Plaid group in line drawings Plate 76
Platters, historical Plate 117
Pleat and Panel goblet Plate 111
Pleat and Panel group in line drawings Plate 157
Pleat and Panel plate Plate 158
Pleat and Panel platter Plate 105
Polar Bear goblet Plate 91
Polar Bear group in line drawings Plate 94
Popcorn goblet Plate 71
Popcorn group Plate 25
Powder and Shot group in line drawings Plate 79

Index

Pressed Block group in line drawings *Plate* 17
Pressed Leaf group from old catalogues *Plate* 29, 29A
Pressed Leaf group in line drawings *Plate* 125
Primrose group in line drawings *Plate* 136
Primrose large plate *Plate* 114
Princess Feather goblet *Plate* 109
Princess Feather group in line drawings *Plate* 112
Princess Feather plate *Plate* 135
Princess Feather (Rochelle) group from old catalogues *Plate* 19, 23, 155
Princess Feather in milk white *Plate* 184
Printed Hobnail goblet *Plate* 72
Prism compotes *Plate* 23
Prism, engraved, from an old catalogue *Plate* 16
Prism, from an old catalogue *Plate* 15
Prism goblet *Plate* 27
Prism group in line drawings *Plate* 13
Prism with Diamond Points goblet *Plate* 96
Psyche and Cupid group in line drawings *Plate* 75

Railroad Train platter *Plate* 110
Raindrop group in line drawings *Plate* 161
Ray group in line drawings *Plate* 14
Ray six inch plate *Plate* 163
Rayed, with Loop border, plate *Plate* 37
Red Block group in line drawings *Plate* 162
Ribbed Acorn group in line drawings *Plate* 39
Ribbed Forget-me-not group in line drawings *Plate* 137
Ribbed Grape compote *Plate* 35
Ribbed Grape goblet *Plate* 27

Ribbed Grape group in line drawings *Plate* 36
Ribbed Grape six inch plate *Plate* 32
Ribbed Ivy goblet *Plate* 33
Ribbed Ivy group in line drawings *Plate* 39
Ribbed Opal group in line drawings *Plate* 147
Ribbed Palm goblet *Plate* 33
Ribbed Palm groups from old catalogues *Plate* 38, 38A
Ribbed Palm six inch plate *Plate* 37
Ribbon group in line drawings *Plate* 67
Roman Key celery vase *Plate* 95
Roman Key group in line drawings *Plate* 94
Roman Rosette goblet *Plate* 109
Roman Rosette group in line drawings *Plate* 157
Roman Rosette plate *Plate* 135
Rose in Snow goblet *Plate* 120
Rose in Snow plate *Plate* 73
Rose in Snow (round) group in line drawings *Plate* 122
Rose in Snow (square) group in line drawings *Plate* 122
Rosette group in line drawings *Plate* 106
Rose Sprig goblet *Plate* 86
Rose Sprig group in line drawings *Plate* 125
Rose Sprig plate *Plate* 124
Ruby Thumbprint group in line drawings *Plate* 162

Salts *Plate* 127
Sandwich Star compote *Plate* 14A
Sandwich Star group in line drawings *Plate* 14
Sawtooth goblet *Plate* 42
Sawtooth, large group *Plate* 40
Sawtooth, later period *Plate* 41
Saxon, from old catalogues *Plate* 20, 21
Scroll group in line drawings *Plate* 140

Index

Scroll with Flowers bread plate *Plate* 118
Scroll with Flowers group in line drawings *Plate* 140
Sheaf of Wheat platter *Plate* 188
Shell and Tassel (round) group in line drawings *Plate* 157
Shell and Tassel (square) group in line drawings *Plate* 157
Shell and Tassel group *Plate* 97
Shell and Tassel platter *Plate* 105
Shell dishes *Plate* 22
Snakeskin with Dot plate *Plate* 74
Southern Ivy group in line drawings *Plate* 166
Spiralled Ivy group in line drawings *Plate* 147
Sprig group in line drawings *Plate* 78
Squirrel group in line drawings *Plate* 100
Star and Feather plate *Plate* 135
Star Rosetted goblet *Plate* 98
Star Rosetted large plate *Plate* 131
Stedman group in line drawings *Plate* 13
Stippled Band group in line drawings *Plate* 107
Stippled Cherry group in line drawings *Plate* 156
Stippled Cherry large plate *Plate* 145
Stippled Cherry six inch plate *Plate* 124
Stippled Clover group in line drawings *Plate* 141
Stippled Daisy group in line drawings *Plate* 101
Stippled Forget-me-not goblet *Plate* 130
Stippled Forget-me-not group in line drawings *Plate* 128
Stippled Forget-me-not seven inch plate *Plate* 138
Stippled Forget-me-not plate, baby center *Plate* 74
Stippled Forget-me-not large plate *Plate* 129
Stippled Grape and Festoon group in line drawings *Plate* 63
Stippled Ivy goblet *Plate* 146
Stippled Ivy group in line drawings *Plate* 119
Stippled Medallion goblet *Plate* 28
Stippled Star group in line drawings *Plate* 147
Stippled Woodflower group in line drawings *Plate* 136
Strawberry goblet *Plate* 142
Strawberry group in line drawings *Plate* 151
Strawberry (milk white) group *Plate* 152
Strawberry and Currant group in line drawings *Plate* 151
Sunburst group in line drawings *Plate* 12
Sunflower group in line drawings *Plate* 108
Swan group in line drawings *Plate* 77
Swirl goblet *Plate* 146
Swirl group in line drawings *Plate* 69
Swirl plate *Plate* 163
Teardrop and Tassel group in line drawings *Plate* 78
Teasel goblet *Plate* 96
Teasel large plate *Plate* 145
Thistle group in line drawings *Plate* 140
Thistle (late) large plate *Plate* 187
Thousand Eye goblet *Plate* 146
Thousand Eye (plain) group in line drawings *Plate* 137
Thousand Eye plate *Plate* 158
Thousand Eye (three knob) group in line drawings *Plate* 137
Three Face goblet *Plate* 91
Three Face group in line drawings *Plate* 89
Three Panel goblet *Plate* 96
Three Panel group in line drawings *Plate* 159

Index

Thumbprint, large group *Plate* 59
Thumbprint from old catalogues *Plate* 15, 18
Tree of Life plate *Plate* 52
Tulip goblet *Plate* 42
Tulip group in line drawings *Plate* 53
Tulip, large group *Plate* 54
Tulip plate *Plate* 37
Tulip (Single) plate *Plate* 45
Tulip Variants in line drawings *Plate* 50
Two Panel goblet *Plate* 160
Two Panel group in line drawings *Plate* 159

Variation of the Pillar goblet *Plate* 28
Victoria compotes, from an old catalogue *Plate* 18
Victorian Novelties in line drawings *Plate* 127
Victorian Novelties, salts and matchholders in line drawings *Plate* 186

Waffle group in line drawings *Plate* 46

Waffle plate *Plate* 37
Waffle and Thumbprint goblet *Plate* 26
Waffle and Thumbprint group in line drawings *Plate* 10
Washington group in line drawings *Plate* 10
Westward-Ho goblet *Plate* 91
Westward-Ho group in line drawings *Plate* 89
Westward-Ho platter *Plate* 92
Wheat and Barley group in line drawings *Plate* 50
Wheat and Barley large plate *Plate* 114
Wheat pattern (milk-white) groups *Plate* 172, 173
Wheat relish dish (milk white) *Plate* 173A
Wildflower goblet *Plate* 123
Wildflower group in line drawings *Plate* 126
Willow Oak group in line drawings *Plate* 159
Willow Oak plates *Plate* 45, 129
Windflower goblet *Plate* 120
Windflower group in line drawings *Plate* 130